EDCO
BUSINESS
REVISE WISE

LEAVING CERTIFICATE HIGHER LEVEL

Peter Caulwell

Edco
The Educational Company of Ireland

This logo indicates important information.

 This logo indicates exam questions.

 This logo indicates the main points you need to know.

Contents

Introduction

This revision book is designed to help you to prepare well for the Leaving Certificate exam in Business.

How to use this book

- The first seven chapters in this book match the seven units the Business course is divided into.
- Take particular note of the study tips given in each chapter.
- Read the sample questions and answers at the end of each section to learn what is required of you in the answers.
- Use the sample Applied Business Questions (ABQs) to understand the type of answer that is required.
- Refer to the glossary for definitions of all the important business terms on the course.
- Refer frequently to the Examination Section (Chapter 8), which provides a course outline, the exam layout, study advice and tips on how to answer exam questions.
- The table on p. 162 showing topics examined in previous years should also be useful in anticipating questions that may appear on the exam.
- Make a study plan for yourself using the one provided on p. 180.

We hope that this book will help you with your revision and that you will have great success.

Good Luck!

CHAPTER 1
Business relations and resolving conflict

edco business REVISE WISE

●●● Learning Objectives

In this chapter you will learn about:
1. Stakeholders in business.
2. Consumer affairs.
3. Industrial relations.
4. The functions of trade unions.
5. The Industrial Relations Act 1990.
6. The Unfair Dismissals Act 1977–93.
7. The Employment Equality Act 1998.
8. The Labour Relations Commission.
9. The Labour Court.
10. Free collective bargaining.

1.1 Stakeholders in business

Business stakeholders

- Consumers.
- Employees.
- Employers.
- Entrepreneur.
- Government.
- Investors.
- Producers.
- Service providers.
- Suppliers.
- Trade unions.

Interest groups

An interest group is an organisation that represents a particular group of people who have similar needs or objectives. An interest group may oppose or support the activities of a business.

Business associations:
- Irish Business Employers Confederation (IBEC).
- Irish Congress of Trade Unions (ICTU).
- Irish Management Institute (IMI).

1

- Institute of Public Administration (IPA).
- Chambers of Commerce.

Trade associations:
- Irish Travel Agents Association (ITAA) represents travel agents.
- Society of the Irish Motor Industry (SIMI) represents garages and motor car dealers.
- Irish Farmers Association (IFA) represents farmers.

Other interest groups:
- Consumers Association of Ireland (CAI).
- Residents' associations.
- Environmental and other special interest groups.

Relationships between the people in business

- Co-operative relationships: Every business requires all the stakeholders to work together towards a common goal for the business to succeed.
- Competitive relationships: Although the business needs all the stakeholders to co-operate, they are also in constant competition with each other as to what proportion each group gets of the wealth created by the business.
- The problem of constant change: The management task is made more difficult by the fact that the world of business is constantly changing.

Co-operative and competitive relationships between businesses

Normally businesses compete with each other, e.g. they may try to offer consumers something better than their rivals, whether in terms of price, quality or service. Competition is good for consumers, as every business is forced to try harder to satisfy them.

Businesses also co-operate with each other in many ways, e.g. milk producers may get together to advertise milk as a healthy drink to increase overall sales.

Causes of conflict between stakeholders

- Different objectives: Where there are differences between the objectives of stakeholders, conflict is likely to arise.
- Negotiating style: An aggressive style is likely to cause an aggressive reaction, leading to unnecessary conflict. An assertive style without intimidation is much more likely to produce a reasonable response and agreement.
- Lack of trust: Where trust is lacking, conflict is more likely to arise.

REVISE WISE STUDY TIPS

Study tips

Make sure you can give examples of:
- Co-operative and competitive relationships between stakeholders.
- Co-operative and competitive relationships between businesses.
- Factors that may change the nature of a relationship.

Resolving conflict

- Non-legislative methods: Using methods that are not based on laws or on institutions that are set up under laws.
- Legislative methods: Using the force of law or some institution set up by law to resolve the conflict.

The law of contract

Most relationships between the stakeholders in business are governed by contracts. A contract is a legally binding agreement between two or more parties, i.e. an agreement that a court will enforce.

Elements of a legally binding contract:
- Offer and acceptance.
- Consideration.
- Intention to contract.
- Consent to contract.
- Capacity to contract.
- Legality of form.
- Legality of purpose.

Termination of a contract

A contract may be ended in a number of ways:
- Performance: Each party does what they are contracted to do.
- Frustration: Some event happens which makes it impossible to carry out the contract, e.g. the death of one party.
- Agreement: Each party agrees to end the contract.
- Breach: One party breaks a condition (an important part) of the contract.

A condition is a clause in a contract that is so important that breaking this clause is the same as breaking the contract. A warranty is a less important clause. Breaking a warranty does not break the contract itself.

Remedies for breach of contract:
- Sue for damages.
- Rescind the contract.
- Ask a court to instruct the other party to go through with the contract as agreed – specific performance.

Key points

Make sure you know the following:

- Stakeholder relationships are co-operative and competitive.
- Interest groups are organisations that represent a particular group of people who have similar needs or objectives.
- There are legislative and non-legislative methods of resolving conflict.
- The elements of a legal contract.

Sample exam question and answer

Question

'A firm's relationship with its different stakeholders may be either co-operative or competitive.' Explain what this statement means, giving examples of the different approaches, with respect to employees, suppliers and customers. (2000, 20 marks)

Answer

A co-operative relationship means that the firm works with the stakeholder because this allows each of them to achieve their objectives.

A competitive relationship means that the firm and the stakeholder may act in opposition to each other because they have different objectives.

A firm's relationship with each stakeholder may be co-operative or competitive or a combination of both, depending on the circumstances.

Employees

The firm and the employees may be co-operative and work hard together to increase the sales of the firm. The firm does this so that it can earn more profits, while the employees want to ensure that their jobs will be secure in the future.

When the firm discusses future wage levels with the employees, they may be in a competitive relationship. The firm wants low wage increases so that they can keep their prices low and remain competitive in the marketplace. At the same time, the employees want a good wage increase to help them to keep up with rising prices.

Thus, parts of the relationship may be co-operative and others competitive at the same time.

Suppliers

The firm and its suppliers may be very competitive in negotiating prices for the goods that are supplied. The firm wants low prices so that they can keep the cost of production down and keep their own selling prices down. On the other hand, the supplier wants the firm to pay a higher price so that the supplier can make a reasonable profit.

The firm and the supplier may work co-operatively to ensure that the quality of the materials supplied is of a high standard. This will allow the firm to produce and sell a high-quality product in large quantities, which is good for the firm and the supplier.

Customers

The firm may work co-operatively with its customers to ensure that all orders for goods are produced and delivered on time. This benefits the firm, as it keeps the customer happy and makes it likely that they will order again from the firm. It also benefits the customer because they avoid delays in production and waiting for supplies to arrive.

The firm may be quite competitive with the customer if they are not willing to pay for the goods supplied at the agreed time. They may charge them interest or threaten not to supply them in the future.

Overall, the relationships between a firm and its stakeholders will be a mixture of co-operation and competition, depending on which aspect of their business relationship they are dealing with.

Practice questions

Higher Level short questions

1. Explain the difference between 'service providers' and 'interest groups'. (2000, 10 marks)

2. Explain the term 'lobbying'.

3. What do the following letters stand for? (a) IBEC (b) IFA (c) IPA (d) ITAA

4. Distinguish between a condition and a warranty in a contract.

Higher Level long questions

1. Evaluate how well the law of contract protects people when they make business agreements. Refer to the elements of a valid contract in your answer.

2. Demonstrate how the remedies for breach of contract can help solve conflicts between contractual parties. (1999, 20 marks)

3. Using examples, describe one co-operative and one competitive relationship that may exist either between or within organisations. (2002, 20 marks)

4. Illustrate the role of interest groups in business. (2003, 10 marks)

1.2 Consumer affairs

A consumer is a person who buys goods or services for his/her own use, not for resale. When a consumer buys goods or services, the transaction involves rights, responsibilities and remedies, which are set out in law.

The Sale of Goods and Supply of Services Act 1980

This law sets out:
- The rights of consumers when they buy goods or services from a retailer.
- The responsibilities of retailers when they sell goods.

When goods are purchased they must be:
- of merchantable quality
- fit for their purpose
- as described
- as per sample.

When services are purchased:
- The work must be done with proper care and diligence.
- The person doing the work must have the necessary skills or qualifications.
- Any materials supplied must be of merchantable quality.

Other provisions of the Act:
- If a good or service is seriously faulty, the consumer is entitled to a full refund, replacement or repair.
- The retailer is responsible for seeing that consumers get their statutory rights.

- Signs or statements that try to deny these responsibilities are illegal and cannot take away consumers' statutory rights.
- Guarantees may offer additional rights to a consumer, but cannot reduce the consumers' statutory rights in any way.
- Unsolicited goods/inertia selling: Where goods are sent to people who have not ordered them, the consumer does not have to pay for them and the consumer can keep the goods after six months if they are not collected.
- A person who buys goods under a hire purchase agreement has the same rights as a cash buyer.

The Consumer Information Act 1978

This Act identifies offences by sellers who give false or misleading information about goods or services. The Act also establishes the Office of the Director of Consumer Affairs.

Study tips

Make sure you know the provisions of the Sale of Goods and Supply of Services Act 1980 and the Consumer Information Act 1978. Ensure that you can explain how they protect the consumer.

The Office of the Director of Consumer Affairs

The role of the Director of Consumer Affairs is to:

- Ensure that consumer protection legislation is operating effectively.
- Inform consumers of their rights under consumer law.
- Investigate complaints of offences under the Consumer Information Act.
- Promote good advertising practice, i.e. advertising that is fair to consumers.
- Advise the government on consumer issues.
- Order that an advertisement be changed or withdrawn if it is found to be false or misleading.
- Prosecute sellers or advertisers over false or misleading claims or advertisements.

Resolving disputes between consumers and retailers

Non-legislative resolutions:

- Complain to the retailer.
- Seek help from a third party, e.g. the Director of Consumer Affairs, trade associations, the Consumer Association of Ireland, the Ombudsman for the Public Service, the Ombudsman for the Credit Institutions or the Ombudsman for the Insurance Industry.

Legislative resolutions:

- The Small Claims Court.
- Employ a solicitor and take the retailer to court.

Caveat emptor: let the buyer beware

Although consumers have legal protection if their purchases are faulty, it is clearly better to avoid these problems altogether. To do this you should take proper care when buying:

- Research the range of products available.
- Compare the prices and quality of the alternatives.
- Read the brochures carefully, including the small print.
- Ask relevant questions to find out about the product.

Key points

Make sure you know the following:

1. The Sale of Goods and Supply of Services Act 1980.
2. The Consumer Information Act 1978.
3. *Caveat emptor*: let the buyer beware!

Sample exam question and answer

Question

Evaluate how effective the main provisions of the Sale of Goods and Supply of Services Act 1980 are in protecting consumers. (2001, 25 marks)

Answer

The provisions of the Act are very effective in protecting consumers in the following ways:

1. They make the retailer responsible to the consumer if they sell faulty goods or services.

2. They give the consumer the right to redress (refund, replacement or repair) if goods are not of merchantable quality.

3. They give the consumer the right to redress if goods are not fit for their purpose.

4. They give the consumer the right to redress if goods are not as described by the seller, either verbally, in writing or in an advertisement.

5. They give the consumer the right to redress (refund, satisfactory completion or compensation) if a person providing a service does not have the necessary skills or qualifications.

6. They give the consumer the right to redress if a service is provided without the necessary care and attention.

7. They give the consumer the right to redress if a person providing a service supplies materials that are not of merchantable quality.

8. The Act gives the same protection to consumers when they acquire goods under a hire purchase agreement.

9. The Act makes it impossible for a guarantee to limit a consumer's rights.

The effectiveness of the Act in protecting consumers may be affected by how well-informed the consumer is about his/her rights and the consumer's skills in making his/her complaint.

Practice questions

Higher Level short questions

1. Explain what is meant by (a) inertia selling (b) *caveat emptor*.

2. List the rights given to consumers when they buy goods under the Sale of Goods and Supply of Services Act 1980.

Higher Level long questions

1. Evaluate the role of the Director of Consumer Affairs under the Consumer Information Act 1978.

2. Evaluate how effective the main provisions of the Sale of Goods and Supply of Services Act 1980 are in protecting consumers. (2001, 25 marks)

1.3 Industrial relations

Industrial relations refers to the quality of the relationships between employers and employees. The quality of these relationships may be referred to as the industrial relations climate.

Causes of industrial disputes

- Claims for better pay and reward systems by workers.
- Claims for better working conditions.
- The threat of redundancies.
- Changes employers want to make in work practices.
- Claims of unfair treatment of workers, discrimination or unfair dismissals.
- Demarcation issues, i.e. disputes about who does which task in the workplace.
- Disagreement about the promotion of employees.
- Introduction of new technology.
- Relocation of staff.

1.4 Trade unions

Trade unions are organisations that are set up by workers to represent the interests of workers.

Functions of trade unions:
- Give workers strength in acting together through the union.
- Negotiate with employers for better pay and conditions of work.
- Organise and represent the workers in trade disputes.
- Help to protect workers' job security.
- Provide services for their members such as insurance and savings schemes.
- Lobby for laws protecting workers.

The role of the Irish Congress of Trade Unions (ICTU)

- Negotiate with employers and government.
- Promote trade union membership.
- Help resolve disputes between member unions.
- Sanction all-out strikes.
- Research developments in industrial relations.
- Provide education and training for union members.
- Promote mergers between unions for the benefit of their members.

1.5 The Industrial Relations Act 1990

- Sets out rules for the proper conduct of industrial disputes.
- Established the Labour Relations Commission.

The main points of the Act are:
- Only disputes between employers and employees are legitimate trade disputes.
- A union must conduct a secret ballot of workers in deciding to go on strike.

- Picketing of the workplace is allowed as long as it is peaceful.
- Secondary picketing of another workplace is allowed only if the picketers believe that the second employer is helping the first employer to frustrate the strike action.
- One week's notice of industrial action should be given to the employer.
- The employers cannot get a court injunction to stop picketing where the union has followed the correct procedures for going on strike.
- Unions and workers cannot be sued for damages related to industrial action if the correct procedures have been followed.

Study tip

Learn the main provisions of the Industrial Relations Act 1990.

1.6 The Unfair Dismissals Act 1977-93

This law was enacted to protect workers from being dismissed by their employer for unfair reasons.

- The Act covers all employees between the ages of 16 and 66 who have worked over eight hours per week for a period of more than one year.

- The burden of proof is on the employer to show that the dismissal was fair.

Unfair grounds for dismissal are:
- Pregnancy.
- Race.
- Membership of the Travelling community.
- Membership of a trade union.
- Taking strike action.
- Sexual orientation.
- Political or religious beliefs.

Fair grounds for dismissal are:
- Worker misconduct.
- Worker incapable of doing the job.
- Worker not properly qualified.
- Necessary redundancy to remain competitive.

Proper procedures must be followed before dismissing an employee, including a verbal warning followed by written warnings.

Employees have the following rights:
- To know the reasons for their dismissal.
- To reply or argue against those reasons.
- To be represented at any hearing on the dismissal.
- That any hearing should be fair.

Actions an employee can take:
- Complain to the employer.
- Complain to a Rights Commissioner.
- Bring their complaint to the Employment Appeals Tribunal.

Remedies the employee may get if successful:

- Reinstatement in their job without financial loss.
- Financial compensation.

> **Study tip**
>
> You should know the fair reasons and the unfair reasons for dismissal.

1.7 The Employment Equality Act 1998

- Discrimination against employees is outlawed under nine specified grounds:
    1. Gender.
    2. Marital status.
    3. Family status.
    4. Sexual orientation.
    5. Religious belief.
    6. Age.
    7. Disability.
    8. Race.
    9. Membership of the Travelling community.
- Full- and part-time employees and applicants for employment and training are covered by the Act.
- Harassment, sexual harassment and bullying in the workplace are outlawed under the Act.
- The Act also set up the Equality Authority.

The Equality Authority

- Eliminate discrimination in employment and in other areas of public access to goods and services.
- Promote equality of opportunity for all.
- Inform the public in relation to equality issues.
- Monitor the operation of all equal status legislation.
- Assist people bringing complaints under the Employment Equality Act.

Director of Equality Investigations

Under the Employment Equality Act, complaints are made to the Director of Equality Investigations. The director may deal with complaints in one of two ways:

- The director may refer the case to an Equality Officer whose decision is binding but which may be appealed to the Labour Court.
- The director may refer a case to an Equality Mediator who helps the parties to reach their own agreement on a voluntary basis without having to impose a ruling.

> **Study tip**
>
> You should know the provisions of the Employment Equality Act and the role of the Director of Equality Investigations in solving conflict in business.

1.8 The Labour Relations Commission (LRC)

- Improve the industrial relations climate nationally.
- Provide an industrial relations advisory service.
- Provide a conciliation service to help resolve disputes.
- Appoint Rights Commissioners to investigate disputes.
- Develop codes of practice in industrial relations with employers and employees.
- Research and publish information in the industrial relations area.
- Assist the work of Joint Labour Committees (JLCs).
- Assist Joint Industrial Councils (JICs).

How the LRC helps to resolve disputes:
- The parties to a dispute may ask the LRC to appoint an Industrial Relations Officer (IRO) to provide a conciliation service.
- The LRC may appoint a Rights Commissioner to investigate a dispute involving one or a small number of employees. The Rights Commissioner makes a recommendation that is not binding, as either party can appeal to the Labour Court for a legally binding decision (arbitration).

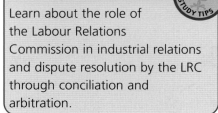

Study tip

Learn about the role of the Labour Relations Commission in industrial relations and dispute resolution by the LRC through conciliation and arbitration.

1.9 The Labour Court

The Labour Court is the court of last resort in resolving industrial disputes. It has three members: one representative of employers from IBEC, one representative of employees from ICTU and an independent chairperson.

Disputes may be referred to the Court if:
- The Labour Relation Commission cannot resolve it.
- A decision of a Rights Commissioner is appealed.
- A decision of an Equality Officer is appealed.
- Exceptional circumstances require it.

The Labour Court will investigate the dispute and then make a recommendation (decision). The Labour Court decisions are generally not legally binding. However, in the case of an appeal against the decision of a Rights Commissioner or of an Equality Officer, the Labour Court's decision is legally binding.

Functions of the Labour Court:

- Investigates disputes referred to it and makes recommendations for their settlement (arbitration).
- Decides on appeals against decisions of Rights Commissioners.
- Decides on appeals against decisions of Equality Officers.
- Sets up Joint Labour Committees.
- Registers Employment Regulation Orders which are recommended by JLCs.
- Investigates breaches of codes of practice when breaches are referred to it by the Labour Relations Commission.
- Registers agreements that are negotiated between employers and employees. Registration by the Labour Court makes these agreements legally enforceable.

Study tip

Learn about the role of the Labour Court in industrial relations and dispute resolution by the Labour Court through arbitration.

Non-legislative methods of resolving industrial disputes

- Workers and managers meet and discuss the issue and come to an agreement.
- The workers can go to their shop steward, who will take up the issue with the manager and try to negotiate a solution.

- Trade union officials from the head office may meet with the management to seek a resolution.
- The employer and workers follow the steps in the agreed grievance procedure that they have worked out to resolve disputes between them.

Legislative methods of resolving industrial disputes

- The Labour Relations Commission appoints an IRO to provide a conciliation service.
- The Labour Relations Commission appoints a Rights Commissioner who investigates the dispute and makes a recommendation (arbitration).
- The Director of Equality Investigations appoints an Equality Mediator to provide a mediation service. Both parties must agree to work with the mediator towards an agreed solution, which remains confidential.
- The Director of Equality Investigations appoints an Equality Officer to provide an arbitration service. He will investigate the complaint and make a recommendation. His recommendation may be appealed by either party to the Labour Court.
- The Labour Court hears a dispute and makes a decision/recommendation (arbitration).

Director equality investigations.
Labour Relations commission - functions.
Labour Court - functions
Employment Appeals Tribunal.
Industrial Relations Act.
Unlegislative Methods

...tive

...is the
...s and
...each
... and
...place
...n an
...el.
...are

...output.
...ty

National agreements

The government invites all the social partners together to negotiate a national agreement, usually to cover a period of three years. The social partners include representatives of the government, employers, employees, the unemployed, farmers and voluntary and community organisations.

A national agreement is a package of measures which may include:

- Wage increases to be paid to workers.
- Actions to be taken by employers, e.g. better safety at work.
- Actions to be taken by employees, e.g. no strikes.
- Actions to be taken by the government, including tax changes, social welfare payments and other spending plans.
- Creation of jobs.
- Development of infrastructure.
- Changes in agriculture.
- Provisions for the less well-off in society.

Benefits of national agreements:

- Provide certainty about the level of pay rises.
- Provide stability over a three-year period, which allows forward planning.
- Saves on having to negotiate several times over at local level.
- Helps to control inflation by preventing high wage increases.
- Improves the industrial relations climate and reduces the number of strikes.
- Helps economic growth and development.

Key points

Make sure you know the following:

- The role of the ICTU.
- The Industrial Relations Act 1990.
- The Unfair Dismissals Act 1977–93.
- The Employment Equality Act 1998.
- The role of the Labour Relations Commission (LRC).
- The role of the Labour Court.

Sample exam question and answer

Question

Evaluate the role of the Director of Equality Investigations in solving conflicts in business. (20 marks)

Answer

The role of the Director of Equality Investigations (DEI) in solving conflicts is an effective one, as outlined below. However, the DEI can only resolve cases that are brought to his/her attention.

1. All business conflicts involving discrimination, harassment or bullying of individuals can be referred to the DEI for resolution. The DEI will deal with discrimination under nine specific grounds: gender, marital status, family status, sexual orientation, religious belief, age, disability, race or membership of the Travelling community.

2. The DEI will deal with each complaint referred to it either by investigation followed by a decision or by a mediation process leading to an agreement between the parties. A definite outcome to resolve the dispute is reached in each case.

3. In some cases the DEI will appoint an Equality Officer to investigate a complaint and to make a decision on it. The Equality Officer may resolve the conflict by ordering the payment of back wages to the employee, by awarding compensation or by requiring specific actions by the employer to stop the discrimination. The decision of the Equality Officer may be appealed for a final decision to the Labour Court.

4. In some cases the DEI may decide that a conflict can be resolved by a process of mediation. An Equality Mediator is appointed who helps the parties to reach an agreement that satisfies both of them.

Practice questions

Short questions

1. List two legislative and two non-legislative methods of resolving industrial disputes.

2. Illustrate your understanding of the term 'arbitration'. (2000, 10 marks)

Long questions

1. Under the terms of the Industrial Relations Act 1990, explain (a) the reasons for legitimate disputes (b) the provisions of the act with regard to picketing. (2000, 20 marks)

2. Describe what is meant by discrimination as set out under the terms of the Employment Equality Act 1998. List five distinct grounds under which discrimination is outlawed under the Act. (2003, 20 marks)

3. Under the terms of the Industrial Relations Act 1990, evaluate how the (a) Labour Relations Commission and (b) the Labour Court deal with industrial relations conflict. (2002, 30 marks)

4. Outline how disputes involving unfair dismissal may be resolved under the Unfair Dismissals Act 1977–93.

5. Illustrate a non-legislative and a legislative method of resolving an industrial dispute.

6. (i) Under the terms of the Unfair Dismissals Act 1977/1993, explain the grounds for dismissal that are deemed to be fair.

    (ii) Describe the different types of redress that are available to employees for unfair dismissal. Illustrate your answer with appropriate examples. (2006, 25 marks)

edco
busines5
REVISE WISE

●●●**Learning Objectives**

In this chapter you will learn about:
1. The concept of enterprise.
2. The role, characteristics and skills of the entrepreneur.
3. Examples of enterprise in action in different areas of life.

2.1 What is enterprise?

Enterprise can be defined as the efforts people make to achieve something new. People have the initiative to start projects, to face the challenges involved and to take risks in order to achieve their goal. This enterprise is important in all parts of a society.

2.2 The role of the entrepreneur

The entrepreneur brings together the four factors of production required for the production of a good or service: enterprise, land, labour and capital.

The characteristics of entrepreneurs

- Good communicators.
- Confident.
- Decisive.
- Energetic.
- Flexible.
- Future-focused.
- Innovative/creative.
- Leaders.
- Motivated.
- Realistic.
- Resilient.
- Risk-takers.

The skills of entrepreneurs

Entrepreneurs need the following skills:
- Decision-making.
- Human relations.
- Identifying opportunities.
- Inner control/self-management.
- Innovation.
- Planning.
- Realistic risk assessment.
- Timing.

2.3 Enterprise in action

Enterprise in the home:
- A family growing organic vegetables in their garden to provide their own food and ensure a healthy diet.
- The children in a family setting up a rota of household jobs to be done so that everyone shares the workload.

Enterprise in schools:
- A group of Transition Year students organising a basketball blitz for the new First Year students to help them get to know one another.
- A teacher setting up a drama group after school so that pupils can write and perform their own plays.

Enterprise in the community:
- Setting up a group who visits and reads to older people living alone in the area.
- Fundraising by the people in an area to build a community centre that is needed.

Enterprise in personal life:
- A person doing a computer training course at night to improve their chances of getting a better job.
- An electrician volunteering to work abroad for a year with an aid agency.

Enterprise in business:
- A city-centre launderette owner starting a new service collecting bags of laundry from people at their offices early in the morning and returning them cleaned and ironed before the end of the working day.
- Two design graduates start a new business producing insulated cloth bags to keep cold drinks cool while people are drinking them.

Enterprise at work (intrapreneurship):
This is where an employee comes up with a new idea for a product or to improve a product, a process or to cut costs in the business. Firms try to encourage intrapreneurship because it can bring great benefits to a business. For example:
- A machinery salesman notices that customers have high levels of wastage of materials and suggests a way of improving his company's machines to reduce wastage for customers. This change boosts the company's sales and gives them an advantage over their competitors.
- A designer in the marketing department suggests a change from plastic to paper packaging for the company's products. This improves the presentation of the product, makes the packaging cheaper and allows the packaging to be recycled by the consumer. The business benefits in a number of ways.

Enterprise in the public sector:
The public sector includes all the organisations that are owned or

funded by the government. It includes government departments, state-owned companies and all local authorities.

- The government's setting up of the International Financial Services Centre (IFSC) in Dublin as a low-tax centre for international banks succeeded in attracting many companies and jobs to Ireland.
- The corporations' and county councils' running of concerts and other cultural events in their parks around the country in recent years is a good example of enterprise by local authorities.

Key points

Make sure you know the following:

- Characteristics of entrepreneurs.
- Skills of entrepreneurs.
- Examples of enterprise in action.

Sample question and answer

Question

Illustrate the benefits of enterprise in different areas of life by the use of examples.

Answer

People need to be enterprising to get things done and to initiate new projects. The same set of characteristics and skills are needed to ensure the success of new ventures, whether these are in the home, in business, in the community or in schools.

Enterprise in the home
Families can dispose of their waste by separating all materials and ensuring they are recycled. These efforts will greatly benefit the environment. Setting up a compost bin can reduce the volume of waste going in the refuse bin, thus saving money on bin charges. The compost produced can also be used on the plants in the garden. An enterprising initiative like this has benefits for the household as well as the environment.

Enterprise in business
The staff in a manufacturing firm start a safety awareness programme to reduce the number of injuries and accidents at work. The firm offers staff bonuses for reductions in the level of accidents because there will be fewer work days lost due to injuries. There are benefits for both the staff and the employer from this enterprising initiative.

Enterprise in the community
The residents' association of a suburban housing estate decides to buy equipment that can be rented and used by all homes on the estate, e.g. wheelbarrows, ladders, garden tools and chimney and sewer rods. This saves each house having to buy and store all of this equipment individually. The equipment can also be used for the maintenance of the public spaces on the estate. This enterprise benefits all the households and the residents' association that came up with the idea.

Enterprise in school
The student council organises a Christmas concert involving all the students and teachers to raise money for a worthwhile charity. Local businesses are involved in providing sponsorship for the event. The students learn a lot about organising an event, the whole school comes together to enjoy a lovely occasion and the charity benefits from the monetary donation it receives.

Practice questions

Higher Level short questions

1. Identify the most important characteristic of an entrepreneur. Give a reason for your choice.

2. Illustrate your understanding of the term 'realistic risk-taker'.

3. Differentiate the skill of assessing risk from that of identifying opportunities.

Higher Level long questions

1. 'The success of a new business depends on the personal characteristics of the entrepreneur.' Discuss this statement, supporting the points you make with examples.

2. (a) Distinguish between a characteristic and a skill of an entrepreneur.
   (b) Evaluate the importance of any three enterprise skills.

3. (a) Distinguish between entrepreneurship and intrapreneurship.
   (b) Discuss the benefits that intrapreneurship can bring to (i) a business (ii) a school. Use examples to illustrate your answer.

4. Using examples, analyse the importance of four different enterprising skills and relate two to business and two to the community. (2006, 20 marks)

5. Describe three enterprise skills required of an entrepreneur. (2007, 15 marks)

CHAPTER 3

Management skills and activities

edco
business
REVISE WISE

●●●Learning Objectives

In this chapter you will learn about:
1. Management.
2. Management skills: leadership, motivating and communicating.
3. Management activities: planning, organising and controlling.

3.1 Management

Management is a process by which plans are made and resources are organised and controlled in order to achieve objectives.

Management skills:
- Planning.
- Organising.
- Controlling.

Management activities:
- Leading.
- Motivating.
- Communicating.

Characteristics of good managers

- Adaptable.
- Analytical.
- Decisive.
- Future focused.
- Hard-working.
- Holders of high standards.
- Leadership.
- Motivated.
- A 'people person'.
- Charismatic.

Study tip

REVISE WISE STUDY TIPS

You should be able to list a number of characteristics of good managers and explain why they are important.

Examples of management in action

Management in the home:
- Preparing and operating a household budget (controlling).
- Planning a family holiday abroad.
- Discussing problems that need to be resolved (communication).

Management in school:
- Planning teacher and student timetables.
- Organising rooms, equipment and materials for classes.
- Teachers encouraging students to work hard (motivation).

Management in the local community:
- A person organising a meeting to raise funds for charity (leadership).
- Volunteers organising the activities of a youth club.
- A residents' association newsletter delivered to all homes in the area (communication).

Management in business:
- A bonus payment scheme to motivate staff to work harder.

- A meeting between management and workers to discuss changes in work practices (communication).
- Introduction of a stock control system (controlling).

Management in government:
- Planning the building of new motorways.
- Introduction of a no-smoking law in the workplace (leadership).
- Charging for waste disposal to encourage waste reduction (motivation).

Study tip

You should be able to illustrate management in action in various areas of life, as in the examples above.

Comparing management with enterprise

Enterprise	Management
High risk of time and money.	Low risk (job security).
Develops new opportunities.	Day-to-day running.
Deals with new product start-ups.	Deals with existing product range.
Deals with long-term finance.	Short- and medium-term finance.
Strategic planning, long term.	Detailed plans, tactical and operational.
Communicating with key stakeholders.	Communicating with all staff.
Leading stakeholders and top management.	Leading managers and staff.
Motivating top managers.	Motivating all employees. Organising resources (human, physical and financial). Controlling stock, credit, quality.
Requires more creativity, confidence, initiative, risk-taking, persuasiveness.	Requires a more hard-working, analytical, organised individual.

Study tip

You should be able to explain the similarities and differences between the role of an entrepreneur and a manager.

Key points

Make sure you know the following:

- Characteristics of managers.
- Examples of management in action.
- Be able to compare enterprise with management.

Sample exam question and answer

Question

Illustrate the importance of management skills in any one of the following areas: (a) the home (b) the local community (c) government department (d) a business start-up. (20 marks, 2002)

Answer

The importance of management skills in the home.

Leadership
It is very important for parents to take on a strong leadership role in the home so that the children will have a clear sense of direction in their daily lives.

Sometimes leadership is given through good example or by being a good role model. The parents work hard and take care of the people around them on a daily basis and expect that their children will do the same by working hard in school and helping out at home. This will lead to the children doing well in school and to the workload of the household being shared by all the family.

Sometimes leadership is based more on the parents setting out clear rules for the household that must be followed by everybody. This more autocratic form of leadership can work well, particularly when children are young, and ensures that everyone does their share of the work. For example, each person is given certain jobs to do each day and they must do them or there will be a consequence or they will lose a privilege. This can make the running of the house more efficient.

As children get older, a more democratic form of leadership may work better where children get to have a say in the decisions that are made. This will result in the children being happier to co-operate with the rules and willing to take responsibility for seeing that they are obeyed by everyone.

Motivating

Motivation can be very important in getting the members of the family to do their best at what they have to do. If the children work hard at their schoolwork and are praised by their parents, then they will be motivated to keep making the effort to do well. Likewise, if one parent prepares a meal for the family and everyone enjoys it and praises them and thanks them, they also will be encouraged to keep up the same high standard in the future.

Parents can motivate their children to make their best effort by offering rewards when they perform well or by imposing a penalty of some kind if they don't make a good enough effort. This form of motivation can work very well and is used in many households. Parents can apply Maslow's Hierarchy of Needs to successfully motivate their children by knowing the type of need level they are at and then meeting this need as a way of motivating them. For example, parents may offer to have a party at the house for the friends of the child as a way of meeting the social acceptance needs of the child. This may motivate the child much more than other methods that are not at their need level.

Communicating

The members of a family have to be able to work together and co-operate with one another, and to do that there must be good communication between them. Each person in the family must have good communication skills and use them so that the household can be managed efficiently. Each member of the family must keep the others informed about their plans. For example, if one person will not be home for dinner, they should inform the others so that food is not cooked for them and wasted as a result.

It is also important that there is communication about big decisions in the household so that everyone's opinion is taken into account. This will help to avoid disagreements at a later stage. Some families have regular family meetings where anyone can say what they want to the rest of the family and plans for the future can be discussed and agreed.

Having and using good communication methods can also ensure that messages are sent and received in an effective way, such as a notice board, home phone, mobile phones, e-mail, etc.

Clearly the use of management skills in the home can be very important, as illustrated above.

Practice questions

Higher Level short questions

1. Give reasons why the following characteristics are important for a manager: (a) decisiveness (b) adaptability.

2. Differentiate between a characteristic and a skill as applied to a manager. Give one example of each.

3. Distinguish between enterprise and management.

Higher Level long questions

1. Describe five characteristics of good managers and evaluate the importance of each one.

2. Select a manager who you know from any area of life and identify the management characteristics they show in their management role. Support your answer with examples.

3. Illustrate why the role of management is important in the home, in school, in the community and in business.

4. 'Entrepreneurs and managers share many characteristics, but their roles are essentially very different.' Discuss.

3.2 Management skills: leadership, motivating and communicating

Leadership

This is the ability to influence people to follow a particular path or direction. In management, this involves:

- Delegating.
- Directing.
- Personal charisma.
- Setting an example.

Delegating

This is where the manager allocates responsibility for certain tasks to a subordinate and gives them authority to carry out those tasks.

Benefits of delegating:

- Tasks are completed more efficiently.
- The manager has more time to deal with important matters.
- Subordinates get trained in decision-making.
- Subordinates get more job satisfaction and become more motivated.
- The manager can see how well subordinates cope with responsibility.

Styles of leadership

- Autocratic leader.
- Democratic leader.
- Laissez-faire leader.

Autocratic leader:

- Likes to be in control.
- Delegates little authority to others.
- Does not consult others very much before making decisions.
- Uses fear to control and motivate staff.
- Places little trust in employees.

Democratic leader:

- Shares power and control with others.
- Delegates authority to subordinates.
- Seeks opinions and ideas from others before making decisions.
- Persuades rather than gives orders.
- Builds up trust with other members of staff.

Laissez-faire leader:

- Lets subordinates set their own goals to a great extent.
- Delegates almost all of the authority to subordinates.
- Interferes very little in how the work is done.
- Places a great deal of trust in the abilities and decisions of subordinates.

> **Study tip**
>
> You should be able to list and explain the benefits of delegating.

> **Study tip**
>
> Be able to name different leadership styles, describe each leadership style and compare the different styles.

Motivating

This is the ability to get people to work hard. Using motivation well, a business can harness all the energy and creativity of its staff to achieve its objectives.

Theories of motivation

- Maslow's Hierarchy of Needs theory.
- McGregor's Theory X and Theory Y.

Maslow's Hierarchy of Needs

Abraham Maslow (1908–70) produced a theory of human motivation to explain how people are motivated. He said that:

- Everything we do is done to satisfy a need.

- These needs can be grouped into five categories, and these five categories can be arranged in their order of importance.
- Once a lower need is satisfied, it no longer motivates and a person can then be motivated by the needs at the next level in the hierarchy.

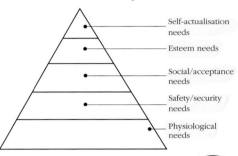

Study tip

You must be able to draw and label the diagram for Maslow's Hierarchy of Needs.

Maslow's Hierarchy of Needs: Explanatory chart

Level	Needs	How a manager can satisfy the needs
1 Physiological	Food, shelter, warmth.	Good wages, overtime, canteen, heating.
2 Safety	Feeling secure and safe at work, feeling secure about the future.	Job security, pension, right to join a union, health and safety systems.
3 Acceptance	Friendship, being part of a community.	Teamwork, friendly atmosphere, social activities.
4 Esteem	Status, respect, recognition.	Job title, company car, promotion, authority, praise, awards.
5 Self-actualisation	Achieving personal goals, realising one's potential.	Interesting and challenging work, career development.

McGregor's Theory X and Theory Y

Douglas McGregor (1906–64) studied what managers believe about their workers and concluded that, broadly speaking, managers are one of two types: Theory X or Theory Y.

Theory X managers believe that most workers:

- Dislike work.
- Avoid responsibility and lack ambition.
- Dislike change and resist it.

As a result, these managers believe that to motivate employees they must:

- Supervise the workers very closely.
- Offer incentives and bonuses to get good work done.
- Threaten workers with sanctions like unpleasant duties, suspension or dismissal to ensure co-operation.

Theory Y managers believe that most workers:

- Enjoy work if it is interesting and challenging.
- Are committed, ambitious and work to the best of their ability.
- Are motivated if consulted about how their work should be done.

As a result, these managers believe that to motivate employees they must:

- Make work interesting and challenging for the employees.
- Try to satisfy the higher needs of the workers.
- Discuss with the employees how their work should be done.

Study tip

When asked about motivation as a management skill, make sure that you refer to the different theories of motivation and how they can be used.

Key points

Make sure you know the following:

- Different leadership styles.
- The benefits of delegation.
- Maslow's Hierarchy of Needs theory.
- McGregor's Theory X and Theory Y.

Sample exam question and answer

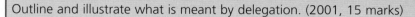

Question

Outline and illustrate what is meant by delegation. (2001, 15 marks)

Answer

Delegation happens when a manager gives responsibility to one of his/her staff to carry out specific functions or tasks along with the authority to make the necessary decisions to make this happen. In addition to the authority, the manager also makes the staff member accountable for seeing that the work is done to a satisfactory standard.

Delegation of some of her workload allows the manager to concentrate on more important matters. Tasks are often completed more efficiently, as the subordinate may be able to give more time to the task than the manager. Delegation allows more junior staff to get experience at decision-making and gives them more job satisfaction.

To illustrate, a factory manager may delegate the ordering of supplies of raw materials to a junior manager and ask him to make sure that deliveries are on time so that there are no hold-ups in production. The factory manager could do this task, but she has many other tasks to deal with and wants to make sure that it will be done properly. The junior manager will see this as an opportunity to take on more challenging work and to show the boss that he is capable of doing the work. With more time to devote to the task, the junior manager may be able to improve on the way this task was completed in the past.

For instance, he may be able to find new suppliers who will supply raw materials at a cheaper price or of much better quality. In time the junior manager may be ready to take on a promotion to a higher level in the firm.

Practice questions

Higher Level short questions

1. Distinguish between the management skills of leading and motivating.

2. Draw a diagram illustrating Maslow's Hierarchy of Needs.

3. Distinguish between democratic and autocratic styles of leadership.

Higher Level long questions

1. Describe three styles of leadership and discuss the suitability of each for managing a restaurant.

2. Explain the management skill of motivating. Evaluate the benefits to a business of having a well-motivated staff. Illustrate your answer with examples.

3. Describe a Theory X manager, according to McGregor's theory. How effective is this approach to motivation?

4. Discuss three styles of leadership. (2006, 20 marks)

5. Describe one motivational theory commonly used in management. (2006, 10 marks)

Communicating

Communication is an interaction or exchange between people that results in the transfer of a message or information.

Elements of effective communication

- Accurate.
- Clear.
- Concise.
- Cost effective.
- Creates a record.
- On time.
- Uses the correct medium.

Benefits of effective communication in business:

- All staff know what they have to do.
- Staff have information they need to make decisions.
- Conflict can be resolved quickly.
- Creates a good industrial relations climate.
- All records are properly kept.
- Necessary technology is used.

Necessary communication skills

- Speak clearly.
- Write accurately.
- Listen carefully.
- Read and understand.
- Use and interpret body language.

- Choose a suitable medium.
- Use communications technology properly.

Channels of communication

- Downward communication.
- Upward communication.
- Horizontal communication.

Factors affecting the choice of communication method

- Cost.
- Speed.
- Reliability: Use a method that will deliver the message without fail.
- Nature of the message or information.
- Confidentiality.
- Record: Sometimes having a copy of the communication and proof that it was sent and received is important.
- Destination: Some forms of communication are suited mainly to local destinations, while others can service almost any part of the globe.

Barriers to effective communication

- No feedback.
- Interference.
- Not listening.
- Technology breakdown.
- Bad timing.
- Unclear message.
- Wrong medium.

Methods of communication used in a business

Communication	Verbal	Written	Electronic
Internal	Conversation Grapevine Intercom Meetings Telephone	E-mail Graph/chart Letter Memo Minutes Newsletter Notice board Poster Report Sign	E-mail Intranet Text message
External	Conference Interview Meeting Mobile phone Press conference Radio ad Telephone Trade fair	Advertisement Brochure Documents E-mail Fax Minutes Letter Press release	EDI E-mail Home page Internet Video conference World Wide Web

Study tip

You do not need to be able to list every form of communication above, but you should be able to refer to a selection of them within the context of a question.

Visual presentation of information

- Pie charts.
- Pictograms.
- Line graphs.
- Bar charts.
- Gantt charts.

Pie Chart

Beef Exporters Ltd
Sales for 2005 by marke

COUNTRY	FRANCE	GERMANY	ITALY	SPAIN	UK
% SALES	20%	25%	10%	5%	40%

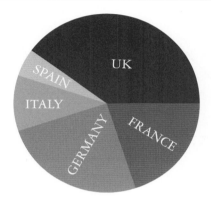

Pictogram

Chez Nous Builders Production Data
Houses Built 1999 to 2002

YEAR	1999	2000	2001	2002
HOUSES	300	700	600	600

1999

2000

2001

2002

Line graph

Model Bakery Ltd
Production hours lost due to factory breakdowns

MONTH	JAN	FEB	MAR	APR	MAY	JUN
HOURS	18	16	32	36	20	18

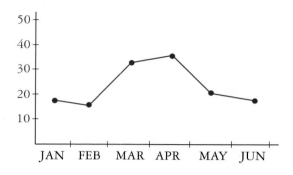

Bar chart

Garden Tools Ltd
Unit sales of Lawn Mowers

YEAR	2001	2002	2003	2004	2005
UNITS	600	1000	1400	1500	1800

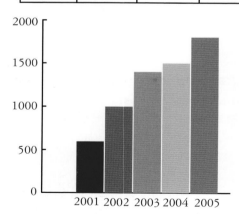

Study tip

You may be asked to draw a line graph or a bar chart. You may also be asked to interpret the information shown on any type of chart, as shown above.

Written communication

Memo

A memo is a brief written or typed message sent internally to one or more individuals. A copy is kept on file, creating a record.

Business letters

A letter may be used for internal or external situations. Usually a letter will be used to communicate on important issues, particularly when a record of the communication is required.

Reports

A report is a document that is written on a specific event, issue or problem. A report presents relevant information, analysis and recommendations to the people who requested it.

A good report should be:
- Accurate.
- Brief.
- Clear.
- Impartial.
- Relevant.
- Timely.

A good report will include:
- Title.
- Authors.
- Terms of reference (the brief or instructions to the authors stating what they are required to do).
- A contents page.
- Introduction.
- Methods (where necessary, the authors will explain the methods. used to gather the information required to write the report, e.g. interviews, questionnaires or tests).
- Body of the report.
- Recommendations.
- Summary.
- Appendices.

Meetings

Purposes of meetings:
- Exchange information.
- Hear reports from certain individuals.
- Consult and get feedback on issues.
- Discuss issues that need to be decided upon.
- Make decisions by voting.
- Plan strategies needed to achieve objectives.
- Gain co-operation and support for a plan.
- Fulfil a legal requirement, e.g. the annual general meeting (AGM) of a limited company.

Types of meetings:
- Ad hoc.
- Formal.
- Annual general meeting (AGM).
- Extraordinary general meeting (EGM).
- Virtual meeting.

Role of the secretary to a meeting:
- Send a notice in advance of the meeting to all individuals who should attend.
- Send a copy of the agenda (the list of items to be discussed) with the notice.
- Ensure all necessary documentation is provided to all participants.

- Ensure all facilities are arranged at the venue for the meeting, e.g. the room, visual display equipment, refreshments.
- Read out the minutes (the record) of the previous meeting.
- Read out to the meeting any correspondence which is relevant to this meeting.
- Take notes of what is discussed and decided at the meeting.
- Write up the minutes of the meeting from these notes.
- Liaise with the chairperson to ensure the meeting is well organised.

Study tip

You should be able to draft a memo, business letter, report, notice or an agenda of a meeting based on specific information or with some details supplied by you.

Role of the chairperson of a meeting:

- Check that the meeting has been properly convened.
- Check that there is a quorum, i.e. that the minimum number of people required under the rules of the meeting are present.
- Have the minutes, i.e. the record, of the previous meeting read out by the secretary.
- See that the meeting follows the set agenda.
- Run the meeting in an orderly fashion and according to the rules of the meeting (standing orders).

- Allow everyone to participate and ensure that contributions are relevant.
- Make sure that voting on proposals is carried out properly so that decisions of the meeting are valid. The chairperson has a casting vote, which may be used if a vote taken at the meeting results in a tie.
- Summarise what has been agreed and bring the meeting to a close.

Information and communications technology (ICT)

ICT is an area of rapid change and includes:

- Computer databases.
- Spreadsheets.
- Word processing programmes.
- Desktop publishing.
- Internal computer networks (intranets).
- Integrated services digital network (ISDN).
- Internet.
- E-mail.
- World Wide Web (WWW) and e-commerce.
- Electronic data interchange (EDI).

Benefits of ICT:

- The speed of communication is increased, e.g. files may be sent by e-mail rather than through the post.
- The cost of communication is reduced.
- Firms can advertise worldwide more cheaply using a website.

- A firm can conduct market research through its website.
- A firm can reduce its workforce and its wages bill.
- A firm can do technical research worldwide on the Internet.
- A firm can automate frequent transactions such as ordering, invoicing and paying wages using EDI.
- Staff can work away from the office through teleworking.
- Travel time and expense can be saved using video conferencing.

Study tip

REVISE WISE
STUDY TIPS

You should be able to discuss the importance of new communications technology for the success of a firm with reference to the technologies mentioned above.

Data Protection Act 1988

The Data Protection Act 1988 was passed to protect individuals when information is kept on computer about them.

Terms used in the Act:
- Data subject: An individual who personal information is kept about.
- Data controller: A person or organisation which controls the use of personal information held about individuals on computer.
- Data processor: A person or organisation which processes personal information held on computer for a data controller.

Rights of data subjects

Several rights are available to individuals whose personal information is kept on computer.
- Access: They can request a copy of the information that is kept on computer. This must be supplied within 40 days of a request.
- Correction of errors: They can have any errors in the information corrected.
- Name removed: They can have their name removed from any direct marketing list.
- Complain: They can complain to the Data Protection Commissioner about anyone who is not complying with the Act.
- Claim compensation: They can claim compensation in the courts for any damage suffered as a result of someone wrongly using information held on computer about them.

Duties of data controllers

Data controllers are obliged to:
- Allow data subjects to access information about themselves.
- Correct or delete any incorrect information held on computer.
- Only obtain personal information in a way that is fair and open.
- Use information only for the purpose for which it was given to them.
- Secure the information from being seen or taken by others.
- Ensure the information is accurate and up to date.
- Retain the information only for as long as is necessary.

Role of the Data Protection Commissioner

- Provide advice and information to people about the Act.
- Investigate complaints from data subjects about data controllers who break the law.
- Registration: Ensure that data controllers who are required to do so register with the Data Commissioner.

- Issue enforcement orders to make data controllers comply with the Act.
- Codes of practice: With trade associations and other bodies, develop codes of practice to help their members to operate within the Act.

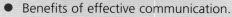

Key points

Make sure you know the following:

- Benefits of effective communication.
- Barriers to effective communication.
- Be able to draft a memo, business letter, report, notice and agenda of a meeting.
- The role of the secretary and chairperson at a meeting.
- Benefits of ICT.
- Provisions of the Data Protection Act 1988.

Sample exam question and answer

Question

REVISE WISE QUESTIONS

Draft a report to the managing director of a limited company explaining the four main barriers to effective communications in the business. (20 marks)

Answer

REPORT

Title	Barriers to Communication
From	Mary Lucey, ML Consultants, Patrick Street, Cork
To	Brendan Fox, Managing Director, Lupine Technologies Ltd
Terms of Reference	To identify and prioritise the four main barriers to effective communication within the business

Methods
We conducted a survey of all staff members by questionnaire (copy attached). We also interviewed key members of the management team.

Main findings
There are a number of areas in your business where barriers to communication are affecting the performance of the firm. I have placed them in order of importance, indicating which one needs to be attended to first.

1. Unclear messages
In communications with customers in export markets there are frequent problems when messages are not correctly translated into the language of the customer or where incoming messages are misunderstood due to language problems. This barrier to communication must be eliminated, as it is costing a lot of time and money to deal with the misunderstandings that occur. Staff language skills must be improved and translators' work must be checked by an expert before communications are sent to customers.

2. Using the wrong medium of communication
Staff have indicated that they are unhappy with the method of communication which has been used by the management on a number of occasions. Recently members of staff who had applied for promotion learned

that they had not got the job from a staff notice board instead of receiving a letter from the firm. Workers also complain that they are informed about the overtime they have to work by telephone call one day in advance. Workers feel this is not a reliable method of communication and that one day's notice is not enough. It is clear that the management needs to take more care to use the most appropriate medium for the message they are sending.

3. No feedback from staff

In general, the staff do not get very much opportunity to give feedback to management. They have to use informal channels of communication and are frustrated when trying to make suggestions for improvements in how things are done. While the business says that it wants feedback, it does not provide the opportunity to the staff. This barrier to full two-way communication may seriously damage staff relations if it is not dealt with.

4. Communications technology breakdown

There have been continuing problems with communications equipment breaking down, causing difficulties in doing business both internally and externally. Even though the firm has invested in new communications technologies such as electronic data interchange, e-mail, Internet and local area networks, it has experienced problems using them due to lack of staff training and poor maintenance of systems. This barrier to communication could easily be corrected so that the firm can benefit from the systems it has invested in.

Recommendations

Each of the above barriers to communication in the business needs to be corrected. I suggest a meeting with you next week to plan for these improvements in communication.

Appendices
Copy of staff questionnaire

Signed
M Lucey

Practice questions

Higher Level short questions

1. Draft a memo, using an appropriate format, to all department managers changing the time of a monthly managers' meeting.

2. Illustrate your understanding of the term 'channels of communication'.

3. Draft a sample agenda for the AGM of a limited company or a club. Supply your own details.

4. List five barriers to effective communication.

5. Distinguish between a data subject and a data controller under the Data Protection Act 1998.

Higher Level long questions

1. Draft a business letter to the managing director of an enterprise, outlining the benefits of improving its information and communications technology (ICT) systems. Include examples in your answer. (2001, 20 marks)

2. Discuss the main factors to be considered when deciding on the most effective methods of communication in business. (1999, 20 marks)

3. (a) Identify the main barriers to effective communication.
   (b) Analyse what a manager can do to eliminate barriers to communication. Illustrate your answer by the use of examples.

4. (a) Define 'communication'. Illustrate the importance of good communications for the success of a business enterprise. (20 marks)
   (b) Evaluate the role that information and communications technology applications play in business communications. Use examples in your answer. (2000, 20 marks)

5. Discuss the importance of good communication between the levels in an organisation. (2007, 20 marks)

3.3 Management activities

Planning

Planning is the process of deciding on the organisation's goals and setting out the means of achieving them.

Types of plan:
- Mission statement.
- Operational plan.
- Strategic plan.
- Tactical plan.

Steps involved in planning:
1. Analyse the present situation using SWOT analysis (see below) to identify strengths, weaknesses, opportunities and threats.
2. Set objectives for the future based on analysis of the present situation. These objectives should be SMART (see overleaf).
3. Analyse objectives identifying sub-goals that must be achieved.
4. Draw up tactical plans to achieve each sub-goal.
5. Review the plan – measure actual achievements and compare to planned targets. Based on this, the plan may need to be revised.

Benefits of planning:
- Analyses the organisation's present position.
- Focuses on future activities so that the organisation can anticipate change.
- Identifies and builds on the firm's strengths.
- Recognises the firm's weaknesses and takes action to remedy them.
- Identifies and exploits external opportunities.
- Recognises threats and finds ways to overcome them.
- Forecasts the various resources needed to achieve the organisation's objectives.
- Sets clear, realistic objectives matched to the organisation's aims and resources.
- Agrees goals and focuses people on achieving them.

Study tip

You should be able to discuss why planning is the most important management activity.

SWOT analysis

To analyse our position, we can use SWOT analysis. This is a simple technique which examines our:
- Strengths.
- Weaknesses.
- Opportunities.
- Threats.

Study tip

You should be able to apply SWOT analysis to a situation such as in an Applied Business Question.

SMART objectives

SMART objectives are:

- Specific.
- Measurable.
- Agreed.
- Realistic.
- Timed.

Organising

This activity involves arranging and bringing together all the resources (staff, materials, finance and equipment) to carry out our plans efficiently.

Types of organisational structure:

- Functional structure.
- Product structure.
- Geographic structure.
- Matrix structure.

Functional structure

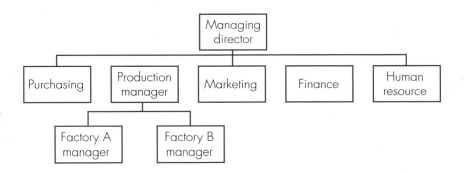

Product structure

Geographic structure

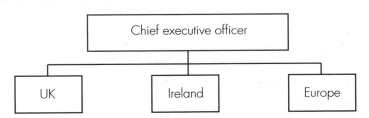

Matrix structure

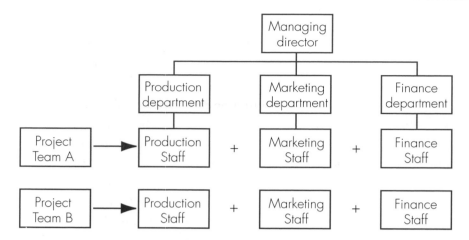

What an organisation chart shows:

- Senior managers.
- Middle managers.
- Junior or supervisory managers.
- Areas of responsibility.
- The chain of command.
- Span of control.
- Line position.
- Staff position.

Controlling

Controlling is the process of monitoring performance, comparing it to the targets set and taking corrective action when it is required. This ensures that the firm will stay on course to achieve the objectives set out in its plans.

Process of controlling:

1. Set out clear objectives.
2. Identify targets and standards that are to be achieved.
3. Monitor and measure performance regularly.
4. Compare actual performance with the objectives that were set.
5. Take corrective action if not achieving objectives.
6. Revise plans to ensure adequate resources are available to achieve targets.

Areas of control:

- Credit control.
- Financial control.
- Quality control.
- Stock control.

Key points

Make sure you know the following:

- Benefits of planning.
- Elements of a SWOT analysis.
- SMART objectives.
- Organisation charts.
- Process of controlling.

Sample exam question and answer

An Applied Business Question is compulsory on the exam each year. Below is an ABQ based on Units 1, 2 and 3 on the course. This ABQ relates to exam years 2004, 2009, 2014 and 2019.

Question

Peter Palmor

Peter Palmor arrived in Ireland from Eastern Europe in 1991 with little spoken English and no money to speak of. He had a university degree in engineering, however, and quickly secured a job with an established property developer in Dublin. His fresh ideas and ability in tackling problems impressed his employer. The managing director of the firm had confidence in Peter's ability to identify opportunities and to learn quickly.

Peter was ambitious and worked successfully for the business, but felt he needed more. His employer helped him to set up a structural engineering and consultancy firm and gave him his first contract. The building boom in Ireland ensured that the business grew quickly and contracts came from other firms that recognised Peter's technical skills and 'can do' attitude.

Peter is now experiencing challenges in managing his business, especially in dealings with his employees, investors and suppliers. Peter seems to be constantly under stress and he is fearful that he may begin to make serious mistakes. He finds that he is working too many hours per day and taking work home at weekends. He wishes to improve his lifestyle.

Over both the short and the long term he wishes to make better use of his time and find effective solutions to his problems. Peter's personal commitment to the business is excellent and he is open to suggestions that will improve the management of his business into the future.

(a) With illustrations from the above information, explain four enterprising skills and/or characteristics shown by Peter. (20 marks)

(b) You are Peter's business advisor. Draft a short report for Peter identifying remedies for the challenges he is encountering. (30 marks)

(c) Evaluate Peter's management skills with a view to his improving his business and lifestyle. Support your answer with reference to the above text. (30 marks)

Answer

Part (a)

Future focused: Peter is focused on future success in business. He came to Ireland *'with a university degree in engineering'*. He is also determined to improve his business in such a way *'that will improve the management of his business into the future'*.

Risk taker: Entrepreneurs need to take risks with their time and money to try and create a successful business. Peter shows himself to be willing to take risks in order to gain success, arriving in Ireland *'with little spoken English and no money to speak of'*.

Flexibility: Entrepreneurs can adapt to the constant change and challenges that they face in business. His employer recognised this: *'his fresh ideas and ability in tackling problems impressed his employer'*.

Confidence: Entrepreneurs have the necessary self-belief and self-confidence in their ability to succeed. In Peter's case, other firms recognised his *'"can do" attitude'*.

Determination: Entrepreneurs need determination to survive difficulties and to keep going when things go wrong: *'Peter's personal commitment to the business is excellent'*.

Decision making: Businesspeople need the ability to make good decisions reasonably quickly to avail of the opportunities that present themselves. Peter quickly decided to take the opportunity when *'his employer helped him set up a structural engineering and consultancy firm'*.

Identifying opportunities: This is the entrepreneur's ability to recognise the chance to start a successful business and to take it before others do: *'Peter's ability to appreciate opportunities'* and *'his fresh ideas'*.

Other possible answers: hard-working, innovative, time management, leadership, realism, human relations.

Part (b)
REPORT
Title: A report identifying possible remedies for challenges encountered in the firm.
From: Joseph Quilligan, management consultant, Main Street, Carlow.
Terms of reference: Identifying remedies to challenges.

Remedies to challenges in dealing with employees

1. The firm should recognise and negotiate openly with the employees' trade union in relation to pay and conditions to avoid industrial relations difficulties.

2. More new staff should be appointed to reduce the heavy workloads carried by existing staff and to ease the pressure of rapid growth on the staff.

3. A new reward system should be introduced to recognise the important contributions of the highly skilled, hard-working staff, e.g. productivity bonuses, profit sharing, promotions.

4. More authority needs to be delegated to staff to allow them to take on more responsibility and share in the management function. This will also provide more job satisfaction for employees.

5. More open communication with staff and more democratic leadership is required so that staff feel more involved in the decision-making process. This will also improve the staff's level of commitment to the firm.

Remedies to challenges in dealing with investors

1. Existing investors, including capital investors and banks lending to the business, need to be informed on a regular basis about progress in the firm.

2. Annual reports should be provided to investors, informing them about the past performance of the firm and about future prospects.

3. Payments to investors must be kept up to date or their confidence in the business will be lost. Interest payments to banks must be made on time.

4. All elements of the firm's business plan should be fully up to date, which will provide existing investors with the information they require and will also be required if additional finance is sought from new investors. The business plan would cover details of the management team, product and services range and production plans, marketing plans, financial reports and projections for coming years.

Remedies to challenges in dealing with suppliers

1. Payments to suppliers should be made promptly and as per agreed terms to ensure continuity of supplies.

2. Quality of products and services supplied should be reviewed and agreed on an ongoing basis to eliminate any problems.

3. Supplier prices should be fairly negotiated to ensure a reasonable profit for the supplier as well as competitive costs of production for the firm.

4. Co-operation on materials and product research and development should be promoted to ensure a viable future through innovation for both firms.

5. Alternative suppliers should be found so that if there is a difficulty with one, another one can be used to ensure continuity of supply.

Signed

Joseph Quilligan

Date   30/5/2006

Part (c)

Peter can improve his management skills and this will improve the business performance and also his lifestyle in due course.

1. Leadership

Peter appears to have strong leadership qualities: '*Peter was ambitious and worked successfully for the business*'. However, he may need to adopt a more democratic style which involves others in the decision-making process and develops leadership and responsibility for completing tasks among staff members. If he can delegate more to others, he will be able to spread out the heavy workload he is carrying at present, since '*he wishes to make better use of his time*'. Alternatively, he could lead in a more autocratic way, keeping control to himself and not involving others in management decisions. However, it would be hard to apply this leadership style with engineering staff who are highly qualified and want to have a say in decision making. He would be likely to lose the key people who would like to contribute more to the management process.

2. Motivating

This is the management skill of understanding others and creating the conditions in which they will want to work hard to achieve the objectives of the organisation.

To motivate staff effectively, Peter could use Maslow's Hierarchy of Needs. He can identify the need level that each staff member is at so that he can use satisfaction of that need as a way of motivating each member of staff to work harder. The five levels of need are physiological needs (wages), safety needs (job security), social needs (making friendships), esteem needs (job title) and self-actualisation needs (challenging job).

Peter could also apply McGregor's Theory X and Theory Y to trying to motivate his staff. If he takes the Theory X view of workers as people who don't like work, then he will take a more autocratic approach to managing, using threat of sanctions to motivate employees to work harder. Alternatively, if he takes the Theory Y view of workers as people who find work satisfying, he will take a more democratic approach to managing. He will try involving staff in decisions, make work as interesting as possible for them and try to satisfy the higher needs of workers.

Improving motivation of staff will enhance the performance of the business and should allow Peter to allocate more tasks to others and reduce the pressure on himself. There may also be a need to employ more staff and to promote suitable staff to cope with the rapid growth in business. This would surely improve motivation for all staff by removing the constant pressure of work overload: '*he finds that he is working too many hours per day and taking work home at weekends*'.

3. Communicating

Effective communication throughout the business is important in helping the business to improve its performance. Allowing two-way communication is important for employees to feel they are included in decision making. Good communication ensures that everyone is working toward the same goal. Clear channels of communication and the use of modern communications technology also make the business more efficient. Peter appears to have an open approach to communications, as '*he is open to suggestions that will improve the management of the business*'.

Ways to improve his lifestyle

- Prioritise tasks and concentrate on important ones himself.
- Delegate other tasks to others.
- Attend a time management training programme.
- Employ more staff or cut down volume of business.
- Find partners to share workload and manage the enterprise.
- He could sell the business and stay on in a management position.
- Hire a chief executive to take on his day-to-day management workload.

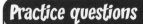

Practice questions

Higher Level short questions

1. Illustrate your understanding of 'delegating'.

2. Which type of management control do you feel is most important? Explain your choice. (1999, 10 marks)

3. Explain the four steps in a SWOT analysis.

4. Name one type of organisational structure. Draw a chart of that structure. (1999, 10 marks)

5. Differentiate between credit control and stock control.

Higher Level long questions

1. 'Planning is the most important management activity.' Explain why managers would deem this statement to be true. Support your answer with reasons and examples. (2001, 25 marks)

2. In relation to organisational structures, distinguish between: (a) functional structure and a product structure (b) line positions and staff positions (c) span of control and a chain of command.

3. Analyse how quality control can assist a firm in achieving its objectives.

4. 'Organising is the most important management activity.' Do you agree? Support your opinion with two reasons and examples. (2002, 20 marks)

CHAPTER 4
Management of households and business

In this chapter you will learn about:
1. Finance for households and business.
2. Insurance and taxation for households and business.
3. Analysing business performance.
4. Human resource management.
5. The management of change.

4.1 Finance for households and business

Cash flow management: Household and business

Reasons for drawing up a cash flow statement or household budget:
- Creates a plan for and allows the control of cash flows.
- Ensures that we do not run out of cash.
- Identifies times of high expenditure (outflows).
- Identifies future shortages of cash so that we can deal with them.
- Identifies needs for finance in the future.
- Identifies future cash surpluses which can be used to best advantage.

Steps involved in analysing cash flow forecast:
1. Examine the net cash for each month.
2. If there is a surplus, there is no problem.
3. If there is a deficit, you must examine the effect of this deficit on the closing cash position for the month.
4. If the closing cash is negative, then the net cash deficit for the month will have to be corrected so that there is a positive figure for closing cash.
5. Examine ways to correct the net cash deficit for the month.

Ways to resolve net cash deficits:
- Cut down on planned expenditures, especially ones that are non-essential or discretionary.
- Defer payments to creditors.

- Try to earn extra income to make up any cash shortfall.
- Spread out the payment of large expenditures over a period of time so that they do not affect one period too heavily.
- Borrow money (overdraft) to cover any cash shortage.
- The purchase of fixed assets should be financed by term loans, hire purchase or leasing.

- Bring in additional cash by getting the owner to invest more capital, especially to finance large capital expenditures such as a new factory.

Study tip

You must be able to analyse a sample cash flow forecast and identify problems and then suggest ways of solving these problems. Make sure you know the methods to resolve cash deficits.

Sources and uses of finance for households and businesses

Short-term finance (less than one year)

	Household	Business
Sources	Bank overdraft Unpaid expenses Credit cards	Bank overdraft Creditors Unpaid expenses Factoring debts
Uses	Buying clothes, food, services Day-to-day household expenses	Purchase of stock Payment of wages Payment of expenses

Medium-term finance (one to five years)

	Household	Business
Sources	Term loan Leasing Hire purchase	Term loan Leasing Hire purchase
Uses	Cars, home improvements, appliances, e.g. a TV	Vehicles, machinery, office equipment

Long-term finance (more than five years)

	Household	Business
Sources	House mortgage Savings	Owner's capital Retained earnings Debenture Grants Venture capital
Uses	To buy a house House extension	Purchase of land, buildings. Large capital expenditures

Study tip

You should be able to give examples of sources of finance to match particular uses and explain why they should be matched in this way.

Current account services for households and businesses

A current account or cheque-book account is one that allows frequent lodgement and withdrawal of money by the account holder. It is the working account, which is used to manage the money of the household or business.

Features of current accounts:

- Chequebooks.
- Laser cards.
- Standing orders.
- Direct debits.
- Credit transfer (also known as bank giro).
- Paypath.
- Automated teller machine (ATM).
- Overdrafts.
- Interest and charges.
- Statements

Key points

Make sure you know the following:

- How to analyse a cash flow forecast.
- Sources and uses of finance for a household or business.

Sample exam question and answer

Question

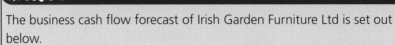

The business cash flow forecast of Irish Garden Furniture Ltd is set out below.

	July	August	September	Total
	€	€	€	€
Receipts	16,000	15,750	14,850	46,600
Payments	28,000	13,000	24,500	65,500
Net cash	(12,000)	2,750	(9,650)	(18,900)
Opening cash	8,500	(3,500)	(750)	8,500
Closing cash	(3,500)	(750)	(10,400)	(10,400)

1. (a) Outline two reasons why Irish Garden Furniture Ltd prepared the above cash flow forecast.
   (b) Analyse the cash flow forecast. Explain and offer solutions to any two problems you think the business may have. (20 marks)

Answer

1. (a) Reasons why Irish Garden Furniture Ltd prepared the cash flow forecast:
   - They wanted to have a plan for managing their cash receipts and payments for the future.
   - The cash flow forecast allows them to identify cash shortages that may arise and to arrange suitable sources of finance to avoid these shortages.
   - The cash flow forecast allows them to avoid running out of cash.
   - It allows them to identify periods when there will be high levels of expenditure and to ensure there is enough finance available to cover this expenditure.
   - They can also identify periods when there will be cash surpluses and decide how to use these surpluses to the firm's advantage.

   (b) In July there is a problem because the firm will have a net cash deficit of €12,000. The deficit is created because the payments of cash will be €28,000 compared to receipts of €16,000. There is not enough opening cash (€8,500) to cover this deficit and as a result there will be a negative closing cash position of minus €3,500.

The firm could solve this problem in the following ways:
- The firm could organise an overdraft facility with the bank to allow it to have a negative closing cash position.
- They could defer any payments to creditors which are included in the payments figure.
- They could spread out any large annual payments such as insurance premiums by paying monthly instead of in one lump sum.
- If the payments include the purchase of fixed assets such as vehicles or equipment, the firm could finance them through hire purchase or leasing instead of paying the total cost up front.
- They could also take out a term loan to pay for the purchase of any fixed assets. This would provide additional cash income to balance out the payment.

In August the firm will have a net cash surplus of €2,750, which will reduce the negative cash position to minus €750, thus there is no problem in August.

In September the firm has a net cash deficit of €9,650, as the payments exceed the receipts of cash. This results in a negative closing cash position of minus €10,400.

The firm could solve this problem in the following ways:
- The firm could organise an overdraft facility with the bank to allow it to have a negative closing cash position.
- They could defer any payments to creditors which are included in the payments figure.
- They could spread out any large annual payments such as insurance premiums by paying monthly instead of in one lump sum.
- If the payments include the purchase of fixed assets such as vehicles or equipment, the firm could finance them through hire purchase or leasing instead of paying the total cost up front.
- They could also take out a term loan to pay for the purchase of any fixed assets. This would provide additional cash income to balance out the payment.

Practice questions

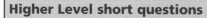

Higher Level short questions

1. Outline two benefits of preparing cash flow statements.

2. Identify three medium-term sources of finance and explain one of them.

3. Identify three long-term sources of finance and explain one advantage of each.

Higher Level long questions

1. Evaluate the benefits of cash flow forecasts in managing the cash of a business.

2. Business cash flow forecast of Ton Ltd in euro:

	January	February	March	Total
Receipts	40,000	50,000	55,000	145,000
Payments	38,000	53,000	57,500	148,500
Net cash	2,000	(3,000)	(2,500)	(3,500)
Opening cash	2,500	4,500	1,500	2,500
Closing cash	4,500	1,500	(1,000)	(1,000)

   (a) Explain why a business would prepare a cash flow forecast.
   (b) In which month(s) does the above business have a problem? Outline possible reasons why.
   (c) Suggest two things that the business can do to help solve the problems. (1999, 20 marks)

3. 'In choosing short-, medium- or long-term sources of finance, firms are advised that they should always match the source of finance to the purpose for which it is to be used.' Using examples from each type of finance source, explain why this is so.

4. 'Managing finance is most important in households and in business.' Identify the similarities and the differences involved in managing finance in a household and in a business.

4.2 Insurance and taxation for households and business

How insurance works

Households and businesses pay insurance companies to carry the risks that they do not want to carry themselves. The money paid to the insurance company is called a premium.

- Proposal: When households or businesses want insurance, they fill out an application form for the insurance company, called a proposal.
- Quotation: The insurance company will quote a premium, i.e. the amount that must be paid to cover the risk(s) in the proposal. The amount of the premium depends on the degree of risk, loading, no-claims bonus and value of the item.
- Policy: If the customer accepts and pays the premium quoted, a policy document will be drawn up by the insurance company (the insurer) and sent to the insured (the customer). The policy sets out the terms of the contract between the insurer and the insured. This is a very important legal document.
- Insurance claim: If a risk that is covered by the policy actually happens, the insured will fill out a claim form describing what happened and stating the amount of money claimed. The insurance company may use an assessor to inspect the claim and to decide on the amount of money it will offer to pay.

Principles of insurance

- Principle of insurable interest.
- Principle of utmost good faith (*uberrimae fidei*).
- Principle of indemnity.
- Principle of contribution.
- Principle of subrogation.

Study tip

You should be able to explain each principle and also give an example to illustrate each one.

Average clause

Besides the five principles above, there is another important rule in insurance, called the average clause. This states that if something is insured for only a proportion of its value, e.g. half of its value, the insurer is only liable for the same proportion of the loss, i.e. half, when a claim is made.

Study tip

Make sure that you can apply the average clause and calculate the compensation payable when a claim is made.

Types of insurance businesses should have

- Buildings and contents insurance.
- Motor insurance (third party insurance; third party, fire and theft insurance; comprehensive insurance).
- Product liability insurance.
- Employers' liability insurance.
- Public liability insurance.
- Consequential loss insurance.
- Fidelity guarantee insurance.
- Pay Related Social Insurance (PRSI).
- Key person insurance.
- Cash insurance.
- Goods in transit insurance.

Types of insurance households should have

- Building and contents insurance.
- Motor insurance (third party insurance; third party, fire and theft insurance; comprehensive insurance).
- Health insurance.
- Whole of life assurance.
- Term life assurance.
- Endowment assurance.
- Pay Related Social Insurance (PRSI).
- Permanent health insurance.

Study tip

You should be able to list some examples of both household and business insurances and compare the needs of each. In a given situation you should be able to suggest the insurances required by a household or a business.

Taxation

Taxation refers to monies collected by the government from people and from businesses, which it spends on running the country and on the provision of services. The tax office is also known as the Revenue Commissioners.

Taxes paid by households

- Capital acquisitions tax.
- Capital gains tax.
- Deposit Interest Retention Tax (DIRT).
- Excise duties.
- Motor tax.
- Pay as You Earn (PAYE) income tax.
- Self-assessment income tax.
- Value Added Tax (VAT).

How the PAYE income tax system works

- The tax year commences on the first of January each year.
- Each employee must pay tax from the wages or salary they earn. The amount of tax due is calculated by the employer and deducted from the employee's pay along with the employee's PRSI contributions.
- The government gives reductions in the amount of tax payable by each person, called tax credits. The amount of tax credits a person gets depends on each person's personal circumstances.
- Each employee is given a standard rate cut-off point by the tax office. This is the

- amount of income that is taxed at the standard rate of tax (the standard rate of tax in 2004 was 20 per cent).
- Any income earned over the standard rate cut-off point will be taxed at the higher rate of tax (the higher rate of tax in 2004 was 42 per cent).

- The operation of the PAYE system involves the Revenue Commissioners, employers and employees in keeping detailed records and completing a number of important forms (Form P12, P60, P45 and P21) that are used to operate the system efficiently.

PAYE tax calculations example 1

John Mayall has a gross salary of €32,100 per annum. His PRSI and levies are 7 per cent of his gross pay. He has tax credits as follows: single person €1,500, PAYE €580, rent relief €200, dependent relative €80. His standard rate cut-off point is €26,200. The standard rate of tax is 20 per cent and the higher rate is 42 per cent.

Calculate (a) his PRSI contributions (b) the amount of tax he must pay (c) his net take-home pay.

Solution

		€	€
Gross pay			32,100
Tax	€26,200 @ 20%	5,240	
	€5,900 @ 42%	2,478	
	Gross tax	7,718	
	Less tax credits	2,360	
	Tax payable	5,358 (b)	
PRSI	€32,100 @ 7%	2,247 (a)	
Total deductions			7,605
Net pay			24, 495 (c)

PAYE tax calculations example 2

Richard and Tracy Peterson are jointly assessed for tax. Richard has a gross salary of €29,800 and Tracy has a gross salary of €33,400. Their tax credits are as follows: married €2,900, PAYE €820, loan interest €480. Their standard rate cut-off point is €48,200. The standard rate of tax is 20 per cent and the higher rate is 42 per cent.

Calculate (a) their PRSI contributions (b) the amount of tax they must pay (c) their net take-home pay.

Solution

		€	€
Gross pay			63,200
Tax	€48,200 @ 20%	9,640	
	€15,000 @ 42%	6,300	
	Gross tax	15,940	
	Less tax credits	4,200	
	Tax payable	11,740 (b)	
PRSI	€63,200 @ 7%	4,424 (a)	
Total deductions			16,164
Net pay			47,036 (c)

Study tip

You should be able to calculate PRSI, PAYE and net pay as per the worked examples above.

Taxes paid by businesses

- Capital gains tax.
- Commercial rates.
- Corporation profits tax.
- Customs duties/import taxes.
- Income tax: Pay As You Earn (PAYE).
- Motor tax.
- Pay Related Social Insurance (PRSI).
- Value Added Tax (VAT).

Key points

Make sure you know the following:
- The five principles of insurance.
- The average clause.
- Insurance required by households and businesses.
- How to calculate PAYE tax.
- Taxes to be paid by households and businesses.

Sample exam question and answer

Question

REVISE WISE QUESTIONS

Ferrofab is a small steel products manufacturing business located in the midlands of Ireland and employing 12 staff. The firm is expanding and the management are encountering new challenges on a weekly basis. It needs to acquire a bigger factory with more modern technology and to hire staff with production, management and sales skills.

(a) Describe what is meant by 'risk management'. Illustrate a method that Ferrofab could use to reduce risks to the business. (20 marks)
(b) Describe the taxes that Ferrofab would be liable for. Give reasons for your choice. (20 marks)

Answer

(a) Risk management means taking action to eliminate or minimise the risks that a firm is exposed to. Ferrofab could reduce the risk of fire to the business by installing a water sprinkler system in its premises that will put out any fire before it gets out of control. The sprinkler system will not stop a fire starting, but is effective in stopping the fire from doing a lot of damage.

Other possible answers:
- *Alarm systems to discourage and detect break-ins and robberies.*
- *In-floor safes to make stealing cash less likely.*
- *Safety devices on all machines to avoid injuries to workers.*
- *Strict quality control to ensure customers are not injured through use of the firm's products.*

(b) Ferrofab would be liable for the following taxes:
   (i) Corporation profits tax: Assuming that the business makes profits, they will have to pay a percentage of the net profits in tax. This tax must be paid by law.
   (ii) Commercial rates: These taxes must be paid by firms to the local authorities based on the value of their premises. These taxes are to cover services provided by the local authority, such as water supplies.
   (iii) Import taxes: If a firm imports goods from a country outside the EU, they may have to pay import taxes on those goods. The goods cannot be imported unless the tax is paid.

(iv) Motor tax: Any vehicles owned by the firm must be taxed before they can go on the public roads. The taxes are used by the government to maintain the roads system.

(v) PAYE: Ferrofab will also be liable to collect PAYE tax from its employees and to pay this money over to the Revenue Commissioners.

(vi) VAT: The firm must also pay VAT on it purchases and collect VAT on its sales. It must keep records of VAT and make a VAT return to the Revenue Commissioners every two months.

Practice questions

Higher Level short questions

1. List four factors that influence the amount of an insurance premium.

2. Illustrate your understanding of the term 'taxation credit'. (2004)

3. Distinguish between a P45 and a P60. (2003)

4. If a business premises had a market value of €450,000 and was insured for €350,000 when a partial loss of €124,000 was caused due to a fire in the office part of the building, calculate the amount of compensation to be paid to the insured.

5. List four contrasting activities in managing a household and managing a business. (2000)

Higher Level long questions

1. (a) Outline two activities that are common and two activities that are different when managing a business as opposed to managing a household. (20 marks)
   (b) Explain three important principles of insurance. (2002, 20 marks)

2. Contrast the task of managing insurance in a household with a business.

3. In each of the following cases, use the income and taxation figures provided to calculate: (a) the amount of PRSI contributions (b) the amount of PAYE tax due (c) the net pay.

   Christy and Laura McGinn:
   Christy's salary is €24,000; Laura's salary is €28,600; PRSI @ 6 per cent of gross income; standard rate cut-off point €36,900; standard rate of tax is 20 per cent; higher rate at 40 per cent; their combined tax credits are €3,900.

Jennifer Cowley:

Her gross pay is €26,000; PRSI is at 7 per cent; standard rate cut-off point is €29,000; standard rate of tax is at 20 per cent; tax credits are €1,900.

4. Watertight Ltd is a family-run plumbing and central heating business. It has a parts outlet that sells to the public and to the trade. It employs three qualified plumbers who work throughout the area using the enterprise's vans. Describe the various types of taxes and types of insurance you would expect the business to be familiar with. Give reasons for your choice. (1999, 20 marks)

4.3 Analysing business performance

Financial information

The trading, profit and loss account calculates the profit or loss made by the business in the trading period. The balance sheet shows the financial position of the business at the end of the trading period. These financial statements can be analysed by users to learn about the firm's past performance and present financial position.

Users of financial information:
- Competitors.
- Employees.
- Government agencies.
- Lenders (banks).
- Managers.
- New investors.
- Shareholders (owners).
- Suppliers.

Trading, profit and loss account

The trading, profit and loss account shows how much income the business earned during the last trading period (year), i.e. the performance of the business. Figures will usually be shown for the last two trading periods to allow comparisons to be made.

From the trading, profit and loss account, we can learn how much the business earned from selling goods and the expenses involved in running the business.

Balance sheet

The balance sheet shows the financial position of the firm at the end of a trading period. It shows all that the business owns (the assets) and all that the business owes (the liabilities).

Assets are shown in two groups:
1. Fixed assets.
2. Current assets.

Liabilities are also shown in two groups:
1. Current liabilities.
2. Long-term liabilities.

Study tip

You should be able to discuss the importance of the profit and loss account and the balance sheet to managers and other users of the accounts.

Analysing financial statements: Ratio analysis

A ratio is produced when we compare one figure with another to measure the relationship between them.

Ratio analysis looks at:
- Profitability, including gross profit margin, net profit margin and return on investment (ROI).
- Liquidity, including current ratio/working capital ratio and acid test ratio/quick ratio/liquid ratio.
- Debt/equity ratio.

Profitability ratios

Gross profit margin: $\dfrac{\text{gross profit}}{\text{sales}} \times \dfrac{100}{1} = \%$

Net profit margin: $\dfrac{\text{net profit}}{\text{sales}} \times \dfrac{100}{1} = \%$

Return on investment: $\dfrac{\text{net profit}}{\text{capital employed}} \times \dfrac{100}{1} = \%$

Liquidity ratios

Current ratio: $\dfrac{\text{current assets}}{\text{current liabilities}}$

Acid test ratio: $\dfrac{\text{current assets} - \text{closing stock}}{\text{current liabilities}}$

Debt/equity ratio

Debt/equity ratio: $\dfrac{\text{debt capital}}{\text{equity capital}} \times \dfrac{100}{1} = \%$

Study tip

In the case of each formula, you need to be able to calculate the formula from given figures for two years. You have to be able to comment on the answers you get as well as on any trend you observe over the years.

Key points

Make sure you know the following:
- Be able to explain the importance of the profit and loss account and the balance sheet.
- Know and be able to apply profitability, liquidity and debt ratios.

Sample exam question and answer

Question

(a) Discuss the importance of the following financial statements to the management of a business enterprise: (i) the profit and loss account (ii) the balance sheet. (30 marks)

(b) From the figures given below: (i) calculate the acid test ratios and the debt/equity ratios for 2006 and 2007 (ii) analyse any trends you notice from your calculations. (30 marks)

	2006	2007
	€	€
Current assets	90,500	75,400
Current liabilities	65,100	44,600
Closing stock	47,300	51,200
Equity share capital	240,000	240,000
Long-term debt	150,000	220,000
Retained earnings (reserves)	60,000	62,000

Answer

(a) (i) The profit and loss account, which incorporates the trading account, is very important, as it measures the amount of profits earned by an enterprise over a trading period. It allows management to see if they have been successful in running the firm over that period and to see if the level of sales has improved compared to the year before. It also shows whether the cost of acquiring goods has increased (cost of sales). The management can examine whether the expenses of the firm have risen or fallen and the effect of this on the net profit. The profit and loss account also enables management to analyse the factors that increased profits and those that reduced profits. Management can then take action to maximise profits in the coming year.

(ii) The balance sheet shows management the financial position of the firm at the year end by listing all the firm's assets and liabilities. The fixed assets held will allow decisions to be made about future increases in production. The current assets and liabilities allow the firm's liquidity position to be assessed, showing whether the firm will be able to pay its short-term debts as they fall due. The finance section of the balance sheet shows the long-term sources of finance being used by the firm. It allows management to see the level of debt capital being used and can show the firm's ability to raise capital in the future. The value of fixed assets may allow management to borrow more money and offer some of the fixed assets to the lender as security for the loan.

The profit and loss account and balance sheet allow the firm's past performance and future prospects to be analysed so that good management decisions can be made for the future.

(b) (i)

$$\text{Acid test ratio} \quad = \quad \frac{\text{current assets} - \text{stock}}{\text{current liabilities}}$$

$$2006: \quad = \quad \frac{90,500 - 47,300}{65,100} = \frac{43,200}{65,100} = .66$$

$$2007: \quad = \quad \frac{75,400 - 51,200}{44,600} = \frac{24,200}{44,600} = .54$$

$$\text{Debt equity ratio} \quad = \quad \frac{\text{debt capital}}{\text{equity capital}} \times \frac{100}{1}$$

$$2006: \quad = \quad \frac{150,000}{240,000 + 60,000} \times \frac{100}{1} = 50\%$$

$$2007: \quad = \quad \frac{220,000}{240,000 + 62,000} \times \frac{100}{1} = 73\%$$

Liquidity

The acid test ratio in 2007 is .54, which is well below the ideal of 1. This has worsened since 2006, when it was .66. The firm may have difficulty paying its short-term debts as they fall due.

Debt

Overall the debt/equity ratio is quite good and the firm is relatively low geared. The debt/equity trend has got worse, increasing from 50 per cent in 2006 to 73 per cent in 2007. However, at 73 per cent, the firm still has relatively low levels of debt.

Practice questions

Higher Level short questions

1. (a) Explain why a firm would calculate the debt/equity ratio.
   (b) Calculate the debt/equity ratio for the year. Show all workings. (2004)

Long-term loans	€100,000
Ordinary share capital	€50,000
Reserves	€25,000
Overdraft	€15,000

2. Outline two reasons why a business would calculate the working capital ratio. (2001)

Higher Level long questions

1. Distinguish between the following terms: (a) working capital and ordinary share capital (b) current assets and current liabilities (c) cost of sales and expenses.

2. The following figures were extracted from the accounts of Lee Systems Ltd. Analyse the liquidity position of the firm using the working capital and acid test ratios. Refer to the trend from 2006 to 2007 in your answer.

	2007	2006
	€	€
Opening stock	10,000	7,000
Current liabilities	34,000	22,000
Closing stock	13,000	8,000
Fixed assets	110,000	88,000
Current assets	50,000	41,000

3. The following is a balance sheet extract for Jackaree Ltd.
   (a) Calculate the debt/equity ratio for Jackaree Ltd.
   (b) Analyse the difficulties the debt position of Jackaree Ltd may cause for the firm.

Financed by	€
Long-term loans	640,000
Capital and reserves	
Authorised capital	800,000
Issued capital	600,000
Retained profits	160,000

4. Examine the following figures for Qute Ltd.
   (a) For 2006 and 2007, calculate (i) the working capital ratio (ii) the acid test ratio (iii) the debt/equity ratio.
   (b) Applying your knowledge, comment on two trends that you notice developing in the business. What action would you take to deal with these trends?

	2007	2006
	€	€
Current assets	76,400	66,220
Current liabilities	48,000	34,100
Closing stock	42,600	29,800
Equity share capital	220,000	220,000
Long-term debt	164,000	108,000
Retained earnings	37,400	31,000

4.4 Human resource management

Human resource management (HRM) is the process by which an organisation attracts, develops and rewards its workforce so that the employees contribute as well as they possibly can to the achievement of the organisation's goals.

Manpower planning

This means planning to have the right number of the right people with the right skills at all times. To do this, the human resource manager must:

- Forecast the future manpower needs of the firm.
- Audit the present manpower resources of the firm, i.e. compile a record of the types and level of skills in the workforce at present.
- Identify additional resources needed by comparing present resources with future needs.
- Make a plan to increase or decrease the manpower resources as required by the analysis.

Recruitment and selection of staff

Job analysis

The human resource manager prepares a job analysis, which includes a job description and a person specification.

Finding the candidates

Candidates to fit the job description and person specification are then sought. Depending on the job in question, the candidates may be found through local job centres, FÁS, employment agencies, advertisements or visits to third-level colleges.

Selection

- All applicants are screened to form a shortlist of candidates for interview.
- Interviews combined with tests for aptitude, intelligence and personality are carried out.
- The successful candidate is chosen, references are checked and the position is offered.
- Upon acceptance, a contract of employment is drawn up and signed.

Study tip

You should be able to discuss the importance of manpower planning for the business and outline the steps involved in the recruitment and selection process.

Training and development

Training

Training supplies the skills, knowledge and attitudes needed by employees to do their work better. Types of training include induction training, on-the-job training and off-the-job training.

Staff development

Development means preparing employees so that they will be able to take on new responsibilities and greater challenges in the future. Development may get employees ready for promotion to a more demanding and rewarding job, prepares workers for possible promotion in the future and boosts employees' motivation by adding to their self-esteem.

Study tip

REVISE WISE STUDY TIPS

You should be able to distinguish between training and development and also to evaluate their importance to the organisation.

Performance appraisal

At a review meeting, the employer and employee should:

- Measure the employee's progress against the targets set at the last review.
- Identify the factors that have enhanced or detracted from the achievement of the targets.
- Agree corrective action to deal with any problems.
- Agree new targets to be achieved by the next review date.
- Discuss the employee's skill levels and training needs.
- Discuss pay and other rewards and adjust them, if appropriate.
- Review the employee's career plan.

Benefits of performance appraisal:

- Encourages employees to reach their full potential.
- Encourages employees to grow and develop as workers.
- Keeps employee records up to date.
- Identifies training needs.
- Identifies candidates for promotion.
- Identifies appropriate pay levels and incentives for each employee.
- Motivates employees, as people try harder when they know they are being monitored.
- Collects feedback on problems within the organisation that need management attention.
- Reassures employees that their talents and efforts are noticed and appreciated.
- Evaluates and discusses the career options that are available within the firm.

Study tip

REVISE WISE STUDY TIPS

Be able to explain the process of performance appraisal and discuss its benefits, both to the employee and to management.

Rewarding employees

Types of monetary reward/ remuneration:

- Wage or salary.
- Flat rate (basic pay).
- Piece rate.
- Time rate.

- Bonus.
- Commission.
- Pensions.
- Profit-sharing schemes.
- Share options.
- Share ownership.

Non-monetary rewards:
- Benefits in kind.
- Job satisfaction.

What determines the level of pay?
- Employee skills and qualifications.
- The supply of workers available – if supply is low, wages rise.
- The level of responsibility that goes with the job.
- Trade union activity will increase the level of pay.

Study tip

Make sure you can list and explain examples of monetary and non-monetary rewards.

Managing employer-employee relations

This is a critical part of the human resource manager's job. No matter how well the employees are recruited, trained and rewarded, they will be poorly motivated if employer-employee relationships are poor.

Benefits of good employer-employee relations:
- Positive attitudes towards work, achieving high quality standards.
- Co-operation: Willingness to respond flexibly and creatively to the firm's changing needs.
- Problem solving: Willingness to actively seek solutions to problems when they arise.
- Positive atmosphere with high morale and motivation.
- High productivity.
- Fewer strikes.

Ways of promoting good employer-employee relations:
- Build trust through honest, open communication and fair dealing with employees.
- Establish and follow agreed procedures for dealing with conflict when it arises.
- Value employees by treating them with dignity and respect.
- Allow for flexi-time work arrangements.
- Allow for job sharing to meet the needs of employees who do not want to work full-time hours.
- Allow for teleworking (e-work) arrangements.
- Allow workers compassionate leave (time off in case of personal emergencies).
- Provide management training for all managers in human resource skills.
- Provide a pleasant work environment.
- Organise social activities.
- Negotiate openly with trade unions that represent the employees.
- Prioritise employee health, safety and welfare.
- Provide canteen facilities.
- Give workers the right to participate in the firm's decision-making processes (otherwise known as industrial democracy).

Key points

Make sure you know the following:
- Manpower planning.
- Elements of the recruitment and selection process.
- Elements of training and development.
- Elements of a performance appraisal.
- Monetary and non-monetary methods of reward.
- How to promote good employer-employee relations.

Sample exam question and answer

Question

(a) Outline the functions of a human resource manager. (25 marks)

(b) Explain five different methods of reward for employees in a business organisation. (15 marks)

Answer

(a) The functions of a human resource manager are as follows:
- **Manpower planning:** This includes forecasting manpower needs for the future, identifying additional manpower resources needed and then planning to provide these resources through training, internal promotion or recruitment. This process may also involve reducing the number of employees.
- **Recruitment and selection** of new staff: This involves preparing job descriptions, advertising the jobs and screening and interviewing candidates before appointing the selected candidate.
- **Training and development:** Training courses are provided for new and existing staff to increase their skill levels as well as their range of skills. Development is similar to training, but it prepares workers not for their current duties but to be able to take on new responsibilities in the future. It is used to prepare employees for possible promotion.
- **Performance appraisal:** This involves the human resource department in regularly reviewing each staff member's performance in their job. This provides an opportunity for two-way communication and may be the basis for possible pay rises, promotion or improvements through additional training.

- **Rewarding employees:** The human resource manager has to ensure that each employee has a remuneration and reward package that motivates the employee to do their best and which is good value for the business.
- **Maintaining good employer-employee relationships:** This is achieved through a range of different activities, such as open communication with employees, negotiating agreed procedures for solving conflict, creating a pleasant work environment, organising staff social events, providing for health, safety and welfare of staff, etc.

(b) Methods of reward for employees include the following:

- **Basic wages or salary:** Each employee is paid an agreed wage per hour worked or is paid a salary which is a fixed amount per month for carrying out their job.
- **Overtime:** Workers who earn a wage per hour for a basic number of hours per week may be paid a higher rate of pay (overtime) if they work extra hours in a week over the basic number of hours. This is to encourage the workers to do extra work when required by the employer.
- **Commission:** A commission is a payment made to an employee who sells products for the business. The payment is calculated as a percentage of the value of the goods sold. Paying commission provides an incentive for the employee to sell as much as they can so as to increase their income.
- **Bonus:** Individuals or groups of workers may be offered an additional payment on top of their basic pay if they reach certain targets that are set for them. These bonuses are often linked to production targets or to sales targets. They provide an incentive to the workers to work hard together to achieve the target.
- **Profit sharing:** These schemes are offered to the whole staff as a way of motivating them and getting them to identify with the profit objectives of the business. If the firm does earn profits, the employees are guaranteed a certain percentage of the profits as an additional payment.
- **Benefits in kind:** These are additional rewards to employees which are not made in the form of money even though they are worth money to the employee. Benefits in kind may include the use of a company car, subsidised meals, free accommodation, etc.

Practice questions

Higher Level short questions

1. Illustrate your understanding of the term 'performance appraisal'. (2002)

2. Distinguish between a job description and a person specification.

3. Outline three areas of responsibility of a human resource manager. (1999)

Higher Level long questions

1. Outline the process of employee appraisal. Describe the benefits it offers to employees and employers.

2. Analyse how a human resources manager can promote good employer-employee relationships within a firm.

3. Draft a memo from management to all staff in an enterprise, outlining a recently agreed method of staff reward.

4.5 The management of change

Changes in the world of business

- Changes in competitors.
- Changes in consumers.
- Changes in rules and regulations.
- Changes in technology.
- Changes in the workforce.

Strategies for managing change

- Managers moving from being controller managers to facilitator managers.
- The introduction of job rotation/job enlargement/job enrichment.
- Employee empowerment.
- Teamwork.
- Total quality management (TQM).

Changing from being a controller manager to a facilitator manager

A controller manager controls employees by laying down rigid rules and ensuring they are obeyed. This is not a good model for coping with change. It ensures that things are done the way the manager wants them to be done, but:

- It prevents employees from using their full talents to the firm's benefit.

- All of the responsibility for managing change falls on the manager.
- Managers may become overloaded if the business faces a lot of change.

A facilitator approach to management recognises that employees will contribute more of their talents and energy to the firm if they are given:

- Encouragement to take on extra responsibility.
- Appropriate training to provide the extra skills they need.
- Advice and support from management where necessary.
- Recognition and reward for successes achieved.
- The necessary resources to complete tasks.

Benefits of facilitator management:

- Employees are better able to handle change.
- Employees get more job satisfaction.
- Managers are freed from a lot of routine decision making.
- The business is able to respond more flexibly to changing circumstances.

Study tip

You should be able to discuss why a facilitator manager is better able to respond to change than a controller manager.

Job rotation/enlargement/enrichment

- Job rotation means moving employees regularly from one task to another. This builds up their range of skills, which increases their ability to respond to the firm's changing needs. It also increases motivation by reducing boredom.
- Job enlargement means giving people extra responsibilities to make their job more challenging and interesting. If employees are open to job enlargement, it is easier for the firm to adapt to change.
- Job enrichment means giving employees not only more responsibilities, but also the freedom to make their own decisions in carrying out their tasks. Employees get great job satisfaction and are often more motivated when they work more autonomously.

Employee empowerment

Empowerment means giving responsibility and authority to employees to complete tasks as well as the power to make the decisions necessary to complete those tasks. It allows employees to take ownership of their jobs so that they take a personal interest in improving the performance of the business.

Features of empowerment:
- Facilitator-style management is required.
- Support and encouragement for the employees.
- Extra rewards to encourage employees to take on the extra responsibilities.

Benefits of empowerment:
- Increases innovation and intrapreneurship among employees.
- Enables the firm to not only respond to change, but also to create change.
- Allows workers to get enhanced job satisfaction.
- Results in higher motivation of staff to achieve objectives.
- Increases staff loyalty to the firm with resultant improvements in product quality and productivity.

Teamwork

Teamwork means a group of people working co-operatively to achieve shared objectives. Matrix-type organisation structures facilitate teamwork.

Features of teamwork:
- Clear targets and deadlines are set for the team.
- Appropriate resources are provided, e.g. secretarial staff and training.
- Choose team members with the range of skills and qualifications needed.
- Team members must have a positive attitude towards working in a team.

Stages in the development
of a team:

- Forming.
- Storming.
- Norming.
- Performing.

Benefits of teamwork:

- More creative solutions are found, as one person's suggestion often sparks off other ideas among team members.
- Solutions are better thought out when a team has discussed them.
- Employees' motivation is better, as they work for the success of their team.
- Team members can support one another when there are difficulties.
- Job satisfaction is increased because being a member of a successful team makes the team members feel good.

Total quality management (TQM)

TQM is a management approach that seeks to involve all of the employees in a continuous process of improving the firm's products and services in order to satisfy customers' needs more fully.

Aims of TQM:

- High-quality products and services and satisfied customers.
- Zero defects in products or services, including delivery commitments.
- Right first time production and delivery, eliminating costly errors.
- Benchmarking, i.e. quality standards that are equal to the best of the competitors.
- Continuous improvement in products, processes and services throughout the business.

What operating TQM requires:

- Constant focus on customer satisfaction.
- Shared responsibility – quality must be everybody's business, all of the time.
- Constant efforts to make improvements.
- Recognition and rewards for success and initiative.
- Stringent quality control at all stages of the process: purchasing, production and delivery.
- Constant review of the TQM process.

TQM incorporates:

- Benchmarking (also referred to as world-class manufacturing).
- Empowerment.
- Quality assurance.
- Quality certification.
- Quality circles (groups of employees who meet regularly to discuss ways to improve product or service quality within their own area of work).
- Research and development.
- Teamwork.

Benefits of TQM:

- Customers are more satisfied, ensuring repeat orders.
- Reputation is enhanced, which makes it easier to get new customers.
- Top prices can be charged for high-quality products.
- 'Zero defects' reduces costly waste of manpower and materials.

Study tip

REVISE WISE
STUDY TIPS

Make sure you can explain how employee empowerment, teamwork or TQM can benefit the business in managing change.

Changes in technology and the role of management

Technology is one of the main causes of change managers have to deal with. Two of the more important aspects of technology are information and communication technology (ICT) and production technology.

ICT

- ICT allows managers fast access to vast amounts of information.
- Databases and spreadsheets can be used to process huge amounts of data very quickly.
- Desk research is made much easier with Internet access to thousands of websites.
- The World Wide Web can also be used to advertise and sell the firm's products.
- E-commerce is used by businesses to sell their products or services to consumers on the Internet.

- E-business is used by businesses to sell to other businesses on the Internet.
- M-commerce: People use mobile phones to buy products and services.
- Bar codes have many applications within a firm, saving time and effort in areas from stock control to the tracking of customer spending habits.
- Teleworking, also called e-work, allows managers to retain valuable staff who prefer to do their work at home and e-mail it to the office.
- ICT has removed the need for managers to hire and supervise large numbers of employees who were previously involved in collecting, processing and storing data.

Production technology and management

- Computer-aided design (CAD) allows managers to examine the effect of any number of changes in the design of a product, at very little cost and within a short time.
- Computer-aided manufacturing (CAM), also known as robotics, is an automated manufacturing system that saves production managers from a lot of the problems associated with large numbers of assembly line employees doing repetitive tasks.
- Computer-integrated manufacturing (CIM) means that the entire manufacturing process is controlled by computer, with very little need for human supervision.

Key points

Make sure you know the following:

- The differences between controller and facilitator managers.
- Empowerment.
- The elements of teamwork (forming, storming, norming, performing).
- Elements of total quality management (TQM).

Sample exam question and answer

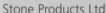

An Applied Business Question (ABQ) is compulsory on the exam each year. Below is an ABQ based on Units 2, 3 and 4. This ABQ relates to exam years 2005, 2010, 2015 and 2020.

Question

Stone Products Ltd

Paddy Murphy was very proud of himself for having set up a successful business. Ever since he left school and trained with his father as a stone mason, he had wanted to own a quarry and building business of his own. He worked hard at everything he did – at school, as an apprentice and now in his own business. He always concentrated on the future and because of this he tried to make the best decisions in the interest of the business.

Over the past 20 years the stone and concrete business had changed a lot, especially in the areas of quality, customer service and in stock and financial management. The changes caused some difficulties in the business, but Paddy's approach was to collaborate with the staff to tackle the challenges. He liked to train his own employees in general, but also, when necessary, to recruit people from outside.

Stone Products's customers were mainly in the construction industry and they returned to trade with the company on a regular basis. Customers were happy with the way Paddy did business. Success resulted from finding out as much as possible before making a decision and having as many of the employees as possible organised into teams and involved in making the decisions. He liked people with initiative to work for him, especially those who would stick with jobs, spot challenges early and find solutions quickly. He allowed his staff to deal with customers directly, paid them well but expected targets to be met.

(a) From the above information, illustrate the enterprising characteristics shown by Paddy. (20 marks)

(b) Analyse the management activities used by Paddy in the running of his successful business. Refer to the above text in your answer. (20 marks)

(c) Paddy often said that good human resource management was the key to his success. Would you agree with his view? Using the information available about Stone Products Ltd, explain your answer fully. (40 marks)

Answer

(a) Paddy shows the following enterprising characteristics:

- Motivated: He clearly had a strong interest in owning his own successful business: 'He wanted to own a quarry and building business of his own.'
- Hard-working: He always worked very hard to be a success: 'He worked hard at everything he did – at school, as an apprentice and now in his own business.'
- Future-focused: He was always anticipating what would happen in the future and making decisions accordingly: 'He concentrated on the future'.
- Flexible: Paddy showed great flexibility in responding to the constant changes in the business over the years: 'Over the past 20 years the stone and concrete business had changed a lot...Paddy's approach was to collaborate with the staff to tackle the challenges.'
- Resilient: Despite the difficulties that arose, Paddy always kept going: 'The changes caused some difficulties in the business, but Paddy's approach was to collaborate with the staff to tackle the challenges.'
- Good communicator (people person): Paddy saw working with others as the way to make his business a success: 'Paddy's approach was to collaborate with staff.'

(b) Paddy used the management activities of planning, organising and controlling to make his business a success.

1. Planning

Paddy shows evidence of long-term planning for his business by training and working towards starting his own building business: he 'trained with his father as a stone mason'. The fact that 'he always concentrated on the future' tells us that he planned on an ongoing basis.

Paddy put emphasis on training his staff as part of his planning for the future: 'He liked to train his own employees'.

An essential part of his planning was the detailed research work he did in advance of making decisions: 'Success resulted from finding out as much as possible before making a decision.'

He encouraged his staff to plan and to anticipate future threats (SWOT analysis), to 'spot challenges early and find solutions quickly.'

2. Organising

He organised his staff resources, ensuring that he had the right staff with the right skills for the business: '*He liked people with initiative to work for him, especially those who would stick with their job.*'

He built an organisation with an emphasis on teamwork, using a matrix structure to facilitate this: he had '*as many workers as possible organised into teams and involved in making decisions.*'

To suit this organisational approach, he adopted a facilitator approach to managing his staff: '*Paddy's approach was to collaborate with staff to tackle challenges.*'

3. Controlling

Paddy dealt with changes over the years '*in the area of quality, customer service and in stock and financial management.*' He clearly used control systems for quality, stock and finance to deal with these difficulties: '*The changes caused some difficulties in the business, but Paddy's approach was to collaborate with the staff to tackle the challenges.*'

In quality control he would have organised product testing, quality certification and quality circles to ensure high quality standards.

In stock control he would have set up stock levels and reorder arrangements to ensure that stock levels were never too low or too high. Regular stock taking would also have been done.

In financial control Paddy would have ensured that there was ongoing cash flow forecasting, departmental budgets and credit control procedures to ensure finances did not get out of control.

(c) In general I would agree with Paddy's view that good human resource management was the key to his success for the following reasons:
1. Paddy's approach was to '*collaborate with staff to tackle the challenges*' that arose over 20 years. Together they were successful.
2. Paddy provided on-the-job training for his employees, which ensured that the staff had the required skills to do their work: '*He liked to train his own employees*'.
3. He recruited externally only '*when necessary*'. This loyalty must have been appreciated by the workforce.

4. By *'having as many of the employees as possible organised into teams'*, Paddy allowed staff to get more satisfaction and increased their commitment to the business.

5. He empowered his staff to be autonomous and to be *'involved in making decisions'*. This ensured that he got full commitment from his staff as they identified with the business.

6. Paddy's recruitment policy was suited to the way he ran the business, as he selected people who were capable of working in teams and who had the initiative to make decisions: *'He liked people with initiative to work for him, especially those who stick with jobs, spot challenges early and find solutions quickly.'*

7. He placed trust in his employees by allowing *'his staff to deal with customers directly'*. His staff responded to this trust by working hard for him.

8. He *'paid {his staff} well'*, which is an essential part of looking after them and ensuring that they will be loyal to the firm.

Clearly Paddy had many talents in running his business, but he understood that without committed and able staff he could not do everything on his own. His human resource management was indeed the key to his success.

Practice questions

Higher Level short questions

1. Distinguish between a controller manager and a facilitator manager.

2. How does total quality management (TQM) help a business? (1999, 10 marks)

3. Complete this sentence: Empowerment helps a business to... (2003, 10 marks)

Higher Level long questions

1. 'Businesses face a constantly changing environment.' Illustrate the truth of this statement and describe the effects of change on the management of a business.

2. (a) Explain the changing role of a manager from controller to facilitator. Refer to areas such as the empowerment of workers and total quality management in your explanation. (25 marks)

(b) Outline the strategies that could be used to successfully manage change in an organisation. (15 marks)

(c) Illustrate the impact that technology has on an organisation's business costs and personnel. (2000, 20 marks)

3. Discuss the benefits of teamwork in a business organisation. (2003, 20 marks)

●●●Learning Objectives

In this chapter you will learn about:

1. Identifying opportunities – market research, product development and break-even analysis.
2. Getting started – ownership structures, sources of finance, working capital management, production methods and business plans.
3. Marketing – marketing mix and product life cycle.
4. Expanding the business, including finance for expansion.

5.1 Identifying opportunities

Ways of generating new business ideas

For individuals

Internal	External
Hobbies, interests	Neighbours, relations, friends
Sports	Holidays and travel
Skills	Copying ideas
Innovations	Education
Business experience	

For businesses

Internal	External
Research and development	Market research
Staff suggestions	University links
Sales staff	Government agencies
Customer feedback	Competitors
Intrapreneurship	International trends
	Import substitution
	Alliances
	Patents/copyrights
	Franchises

Study tip

REVISE WISE
STUDY TIPS

You will not be required to know long lists of sources of business ideas, but you should be able to illustrate with a few examples of each type.

Market research

Market research is the process of collecting and analysing information about the market for a product. This helps a business to make the right decisions about bringing products to the market so that they will meet consumer needs.

Information sought through market research:
- The size of the market.
- Consumer profile in terms of age, gender, income, lifestyles, tastes and preferences.
- Competitors – their products, market share and prices.
- Consumer reaction to a new product – its price, design features, performance and appearance.
- Market trends, i.e. changes in fashions or consumer preferences.

Importance of market research information:
- Quantifies the market and identifies the target market for the product.
- Ensures the company's product meets consumer needs in terms of product features, quality and price.

- Saves money by stopping the development of a new product if it is not likely to be viable in the marketplace.
- Allows the firm to devise marketing strategies that emphasise the product's unique selling points.
- The firm can exploit competitors' weaknesses and counteract their strengths.
- The firm can evaluate the effectiveness of its promotional activities.
- The firm can anticipate trends and changes that are happening in the market.

Study tip

REVISE WISE
STUDY TIPS

You should be able to discuss the reasons for conducting market research and also the type of information that is sought in market research.

Methods of market research:
- Desk research: This type of research is based on information that has already been assembled by others. This information can be taken from a variety of sources, both internal and external.
- Field research: This type of market research involves going out into the marketplace and finding the information you require yourself.

Study tip

REVISE WISE
STUDY TIPS

Make sure you can describe or evaluate both types of market research methods.

The development process for a new product/service

- Stage 1: Idea generation.
- Stage 2: Screening of product ideas.
- Stage 3: Concept development.
- Stage 4: Feasibility study.
- Stage 5: Prototype development.
- Stage 6: Test marketing.
- Stage 7: Commercial production and product launch.

Study tip

REVISE WISE STUDY TIPS

You need to be able to list the stages in product development and explain and illustrate each stage with an example.

Formulae for break-even analysis

- total revenue = quantity sold × unit price
- total costs = fixed costs + variable costs
- contribution per unit = selling price − variable cost per unit

To find the break-even point:

$$\frac{\text{fixed costs}}{\text{contribution per unit}} = \text{units}$$

To find the margin of safety:

target output − break-even point = units

Break-even analysis

For a product to break even it must earn enough money from sales revenues to cover all of the costs involved in production. The break-even point is the level of production at which total sales revenue equals total costs. The break-even point can be found by using a formula or by drawing a break-even chart.

Finding the break-even point using a break-even chart

A break-even chart will show:
- All of the costs and revenues of the firm in visual form.
- The break-even point where total costs = total revenues.
- The margin of safety.

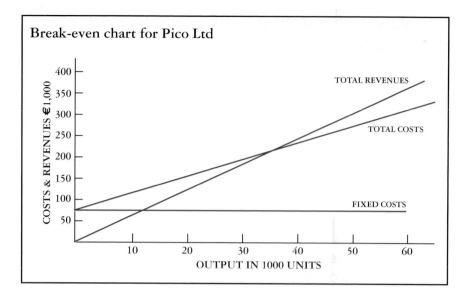

Break-even chart for Pico Ltd

At each level of output we can read the following from the chart:

- Fixed costs, from the fixed costs line.
- Total costs, from the total costs line.
- Variable costs (total cost – fixed cost).
- Revenues that would be earned, from the total revenue line.
- Losses (if output is below the BEP).
- Profits (if output is above the BEP)

Study tip

You should be able to draw a break-even chart from a set of figures given to you. Careful labelling of the diagram is important. Make sure that you can explain the importance (uses) of a break-even chart.

Sources of assistance in developing new products

- Advice, information, facilities and resources are available from Enterprise Ireland, chambers of commerce and business incubation centres.
- Enterprise Ireland operates an Enterprise Link Unit, which is dedicated to directing entrepreneurs towards the information and assistance they need to successfully develop their products.
- Feasibility study grants are available from a number of agencies to assist in the development of new products, such as County Enterprise Boards, Area Partnership Companies and the LEADER Plus programme.

Key points

Make sure you know the following:

- Sources of business opportunities.
- Methods of market research.
- Stages in developing a new product.
- How to apply break-even analysis.

Sample exam question and answer

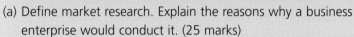

Question

(a) Define market research. Explain the reasons why a business enterprise would conduct it. (25 marks)

(b) Analyse two market research techniques for a product or service of your choice. (2004, 20 marks)

Answer

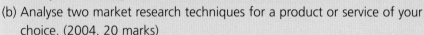

(a) Market research is the process of gathering relevant information on the market for a product or service to allow the firm to make better marketing decisions.

An enterprise would conduct market research for the following reasons:

- To quantify the size of the market so that the firm can estimate its potential sales.
- To identify trends in the market so that the firm can take action to respond to new trends.
- To find out consumer reactions to new products that the firm is developing.
- To find out the target market for the product so that the right marketing strategies can be used.
- To quantify the effects of recent advertising or promotional activities on consumers' spending patterns.
- To find out about competitors and the strengths and weaknesses of their products so that the firm can respond appropriately.
- To find out what shares of the market the firm and its competitors have.
- To gather the market information needed for marketing planning and to develop effective marketing strategies.

(b)

(1) Desk research
- A firm can use desk research for a new healthy yoghurt drink that it plans to add to its product range.
- The firm can research its own sales and marketing reports of recent years to confirm a growing demand among consumers for such a product.
- The firm can read market reports from trade magazines to confirm the existence of a market for their new product.
- The Internet can be used to research international trends and information on similar products launched successfully in other markets.
- The firm can quantify the potential market by examining the results of the census on the young section of the population at the Central Statistics Office.

(2) Field research
- The firm could also use field research to discover the potential market for its new product.
- A customer survey using a specially devised questionnaire can get very specific information from individual consumers about their tastes, preferences and their reaction to the product.
- Interviews with consumers can also provide qualitative information about consumers' attitudes to the product.
- Product sampling combined with interviews could produce real consumer feedback on how they found the product and their future intentions to purchase.
- In field research, the firm can get a truly representative sample of people who reflect the market for the product.
- Observation of consumers and their purchasing behaviour in retail outlets gives the firm information on actual purchases rather than intention to purchase.

Practice questions

Higher Level short questions

1. Define market research. (2001, 10 marks)

2. What does prototype development involve? (2001, 10 marks)

3. Define the term 'feasibility study'. (1999, 10 marks)

Higher Level long questions

1. Illustrate two internal and two external sources of new product or service ideas. (2003, 25 marks)

2. Analyse the development process of a new product/service of your choice under the following headings: (a) ideas generation (b) product/service screening (c) concept development (d) feasibility study (e) prototype development. (2000, 60 marks)

3. KPL Ltd, a manufacturer of clay plant pots, provides the following figures in relation to a new product it plans to start producing: target output (sales) 8,000 units; full capacity output 10,000 units; variable cost per unit €16; selling price per unit €22; fixed costs €33,000. Use a break-even chart to show: (a) the break-even point (b) the profit the company would make at full capacity (c) the margin of safety at the target output (d) the losses at an output of 4,000 units.

4. Seatsoft Ltd manufactures office chairs. To survive it must meet its costs. Seatsoft supplies the following figures about its activities: fixed costs €1 million; variable costs per unit €20; forecast output (sales) 70,000 units; selling price €40 per unit. By means of a break-even chart, illustrate: (a) the break-even point (b) the profit at full capacity (c) the margin of safety. (2001, 40 marks)

5.2 Getting started

Reasons for starting a new business

- For some people, being an employee does not offer enough challenge, but making a successful new business does.
- Many people have a strong desire to make their own decisions.
- Setting up a business offers the chance of earning profits.
- Some people feel more secure controlling their own business.
- Sometimes people are pushed into setting up a business by circumstances, e.g. a redundant worker with a lump sum of money may start a new business as a way of self-employment.
- Some people can come up with new ideas or inventions which become the basis for a business.

Challenges facing new businesses

- It can take a long time and a lot of money to get the product ready for sale on the market.
- It can be difficult to obtain start-up finance.
- Many promising new businesses fail because of cash flow problems.
- Getting the product onto retailers' shelves is essential to success, but this can be difficult for a start-up business.
- New businesses usually have to compete with long-established businesses.
- Finding the right staff and training them can be difficult.
- Finding suitable premises at a reasonable rent from which to run the business.
- Legal requirements, e.g. getting a licence, getting planning permission, registering for tax or forming a limited company.

Study tip

You should be able to discuss the reasons why people start their own business and also to explain the challenges faced by new firms.

Ownership structures

- Sole trader.
- Partnership.
- Private limited company.
- Co-operative.
- Public limited company (PLC). (See also pp. 116–20.)

Study tip

Make sure that you can compare the different types of ownership structures in terms of their suitability for a new business.

Sources of finance for new businesses

Type of finance	Uses
Long term (5+ years): Owner's capital (equity) Loans/debentures Venture capital Grants	Fixed assets
Medium term (1–5 years): Term loan Leasing Hire purchase	Vehicles, equipment
Short term (0–1 year): Trade credit Overdraft Factoring debtors Accrued expenses	Stock, expenses

Study tip

You need to be able to differentiate between long-, medium- and short-term sources of finance and match each source with the purpose for which it is being used.

Managing working capital

Working capital refers to the assets and finance available to be used in the day-to-day running of the business.

working capital =
current assets − current liabilities

Methods of managing working capital:
- Cash flow forecasting.
- Credit control.
- Liquidity ratios.
- Stock control.

Methods of production

- Job production: Each item is produced individually for a specific customer and to that customer's specific requirements, e.g. a one-off trophy, a made-to-measure wedding dress, a ship or a landscape gardening service.
- Batch production: Producing a quantity of a product at one time and then switching production to a different product, e.g. clothing and footwear, which are produced in batches of different sizes, styles, materials and colours.
- Mass production: Producing very large quantities of identical products by a continuous automated process, e.g. biros, razors, computer chips, cigarettes and cars.

Study tip

As well as being able to describe each method of production, you should also be able to illustrate them by referring to examples.

Elements of a business plan:
- Nature of the business.
- Ownership (description of the owners and the legal structure of the business).
- Management.
- Marketing plan.
- Production plan.
- Financial plan.

Business plan

Just like any other business, a new business must have a business plan. The business plan sets out the firm's objectives and the methods and resources it will use to achieve these objectives.

Study tip

Know the main headings for a business plan. You should be able to draw up a business plan using information provided to you.

Key points

Make sure you know the following:
- Challenges facing new businesses.
- Ownership structures.
- Sources of finance.
- Elements of a business plan.

Sample exam question and answer

Question

Michael Kelly is 29 years old and is a graduate with an engineering degree. He has been working in the area of research and development in a large transnational company since graduation. He has a desire to work for himself and feels that the time is right to form his own business in his home town producing electronic parts for domestic appliances. He has asked you to help him in writing his business plan.

(a) Explain the importance of a business plan. (20 marks)
(b) Draft a business plan for Michael Kelly's venture under five main headings. State relevant assumptions where necessary. (2002, 40 marks)

Answer

(a) A business plan is important for the following reasons:
- To give a clear focus to management and all other employees on achieving the objectives of the firm.
- To have objectives against which the actual performance of the firm can be measured.
- In drawing up the plan, the promoters can evaluate whether the business is a viable one.
- The plan is needed to convince prospective investors that the firm is likely to be a success.
- A business plan is necessary to show to banks when seeking loan finance from them.
- The government will want to see a business plan when considering giving grants to the business.
- To provide information on the firm to other interested parties, such as employees, trade unions and suppliers.

(b)

BUSINESS PLAN

MK Engineering Ltd, Domo Industrial Estate, Nenagh, Co. Tipperary

The business

MK Engineering manufactures electronic parts for supply to manufacturers of domestic appliances worldwide. The firm is set to take advantage of the strong growth in the world market for electrical appliances. The firm has been registered as a private limited company.

Ownership and management team
- Shareholders: Michael Kelly, James Wilson, Patrick McElroy.
- Managing director: Michael Kelly, graduate in engineering, taking responsibility for product development.
- Production manager: Emily O'Loughlin, Bachelor of Production Engineering.
- Marketing director: James Wilson, MBA (Marketing).
- Finance manager: Gordon Allen, ACCA.

Production plan

Production based at Nenagh factory with initial staff of 30 operatives. The range of products will be produced on a batch production basis. Some products will be outsourced from the UK until the plant reaches full production. There is a supply of suitably qualified staff available in the region around the factory. Initially the plant will operate two production shifts a day with the option of adding a third shift. There is adequate land to extend the factory in the medium term.

97

Marketing plan

The firm has already secured a five-year contract to supply parts to German multinational manufacturer Kuhne, for whom Michael Kelly previously worked. The firm intends to develop markets with major appliance manufacturers in Europe, the Far East and in the United States. Product innovation is seen as the firm's unique selling point in competing in the marketplace. The firm's pricing will be competitive with the other manufacturers, but we will have an advantage in superior quality and reliable performance. Our main method in promoting our products will be in specialised trade exhibitions around the world.

Financial plan

Finance required	Source
Long-term capital: €5 million	€1.5 million share capital issued
	€1.5 million government grants
	€2 million 20-year bank loan
Medium-term capital: €250,000	Vehicles hire purchase: €100,000
	Equipment leasing: €150,000
Short-term capital: €100,000	Bank overdraft: €100,000

Detailed cash flow forecasts and projected final accounts for the first three years are attached. Projected profits are year one €200,000; year two €300,000; year three €500,000.

Practice questions

Higher Level short questions

1. List two short-term and three long-term sources of finance suitable for a new business enterprise.

2. Outline four challenges a new start-up business may have to overcome.

3. List five headings usually contained in a business plan.

Higher Level long questions

1. Outline the reasons why people set up in business and the problems they encounter in doing so.

2. Discuss the benefits and drawbacks to a start-up business of using (a) equity capital (b) debt capital.

3. Explain why you would recommend a private limited company as a type of business organisation for a new business venture. (2004, 20 marks)

5.3 Marketing

Marketing is the process of identifying the needs of consumers and producing and selling products to satisfy those needs profitably.

The marketing concept requires the firm to first identify the needs of the consumer and then develop products to satisfy those needs in a way that will be profitable for the firm.

> **Study tip**
>
> *REVISE WISE STUDY TIPS*
>
> The marketing concept is a key idea that you should be able to explain and refer to in your answers on marketing.

Marketing strategy

Elements of the marketing strategy:

- Market segmentation: Within each market there may be a number of different market segments.
- Target markets: A target market may be defined by characteristics such as age, gender, lifestyle and income level.
- Product portfolio: The range of products marketed by a firm is called a product portfolio.
- Product positioning: Choosing the product's image relative to its competitors in the marketplace. Once the product's positioning in the market has been decided, all of the elements of the marketing mix are chosen to support that position.
- Marketing mix: The combination of product, price, place and promotion.

Marketing mix

The marketing mix has four elements that are aimed at achieving the firm's marketing goals:

- Product.
- Price.
- Place.
- Promotion.

Product

The product is what the consumer buys to satisfy their needs. There are many different aspects to the product in marketing terms.

- Core of the product: The main function of the product.
- Augmented product: Includes all of the extra features which help to sell the product, e.g. brand name, image, style, reputation, packaging, quality, service, guarantee, etc.
- Unique selling point (USP): A feature that distinguishes the product from its competitors.
- Design function: The product must be designed to reliably do what it is supposed to do in order to satisfy the core needs of its target market.

- Design form: The product must also satisfy the target market's augmented needs in terms of shape, style, colour and image.
- Branding and packaging are also important elements of the product's identity.

Product life cycle

The product life cycle illustrates how the sales of a product rise and fall over its lifetime, from its initial introduction to decline and eventual withdrawal from the market. The timescale of a product's life cycle can vary greatly, from a few weeks to many years.

Stages in the product life cycle:
- Development: When a new product is being prepared for introduction to the market, no income is earned but money is spent on research and development, prototypes and market research.
- Introduction: The product is launched onto the market. Sales are usually slow until the product becomes well known.
- Growth: As the advertising campaign takes effect, sales of the product increase rapidly.
- Maturity: The rate of increase in sales starts to slow down.
- Saturation: Sales have levelled off because most consumers in the target market are already buying the product.
- Decline: The product has outlived the market demand for it.

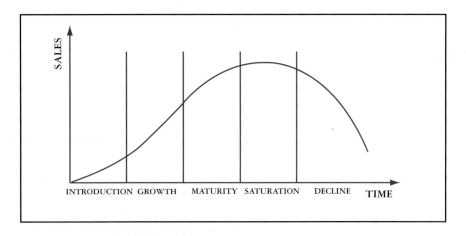

Study tip

You must be able to reproduce the diagram on the product life cycle and explain each stage.

Price

The price of a product must cover all the firm's costs and also earn profits. It must be competitive with other products on the market so that they can get a high level of sales. The price chosen is also part of the product's image and its positioning in the market.

Pricing strategies and tactics:
- Cost plus pricing.
- Loss leaders/below-cost selling.
- Penetration pricing.
- Predatory pricing.
- Premium pricing.
- Price discounting.
- Price discrimination.
- Price skimming.

Factors that determine price:
- Cost of production.
- Demand for the product.
- Price strategy.
- Competitors' prices.
- Stage in the product's life cycle.

Place

This element of the marketing mix relates to the range of market mechanisms and distribution channels that are used to ensure that the product is available to the consumer in as many different locations as possible so that they can conveniently purchase it.

Channels of distribution

This is the network of firms that distribute and deliver goods from manufacturer to consumer.
- Producer→wholesalers→retailers→consumers: Producers sell in large quantities to wholesalers, who store the goods in warehouses and sell a wide range of products to retailers. Retailers then sell the goods to individual consumers.

- Producer→retailers→consumers: The retailer buys large quantities of products directly from the producers at relatively cheap prices. This channel suits mail order retailers that issue catalogues, e.g. Argos.
- Producer→consumers: Producers sell their products directly to consumers, e.g. fitted kitchen manufacturers, craft manufacturers who sell from their workshops, factories that sell direct from factory shops or producers who deliver products like bread and vegetables direct to customers.

Study tip

You must be able to illustrate three different channels of distribution with simple diagrams and identify a product each channel would be suited to.

Wholesalers

Traditional wholesalers are companies that buy goods in large quantities from manufacturers, store them and sell them in turn to retailers.

Cash and carry wholesalers are businesses where the retailers come and select their own goods, pay for them immediately and transport them home in their own vehicles. Prices in cash and carry wholesalers are usually lower than in traditional wholesalers.

Promotion

Promotion involves a range of activities, e.g. advertising, sales promotion and public relations, whereby the firm tries to influence the target market to purchase its product.

Advertising

Advertising is a direct communication to a target market, usually with the aim of persuading them to buy a product.

Functions of advertising:
- Compete.
- Create consumer loyalty.
- Increase the market.
- Inform.
- Persuade.
- Remind.

Advertising media include:
- Television.
- Radio.
- Newspapers.
- Magazines.
- Posters.
- Internet.
- Cinema.
- Direct mail.

To be successful, an advertisement must take the consumer through four stages: attention, interest, desire, action (AIDA).

Sales promotion

'Sales promotion' is the term used to describe a wide range of activities that aim to boost the sales of products in the short term. In particular, they try to attract customers who usually use other brands with a view to convincing them to change brand permanently.

Sales promotion methods:
- Free samples.
- Reduced-price offers (50 cent off).
- Bonus offers (20 per cent extra free).
- Competitions.
- Free draws.
- Stamp or coupon saving schemes.
- Money-off coupons.
- Merchandising, where in-store product displays are made to attract attention to the product.
- Joint promotions, where two products are sold together.
- Direct marketing is a sales promotion wherepromotional materials are sent direct to individual customers.

Public relations

The aim of public relations is to create and maintain a good image of the firm and its products. The person in the business who manages public relations is usually called a public relations officer (PRO).

Public relations methods:
- Company magazines.
- Corporate identity, e.g. company logo, corporate colours, staff uniforms or dress code.

- Corporate websites.
- Factory visits by tourists or school groups.
- Press conferences.
- Press releases.
- Sponsorships.

Study tip

You should be able to illustrate the application of the four elements of the marketing mix to a product or service of your choice.

Key points

Make sure you know the following:
- Marketing concept.
- Marketing strategy.
- Marketing mix (product, price, place, promotion).
- Product life cycle (including the diagram).

Sample exam question and answer

Question
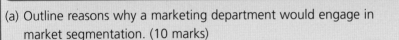

(a) Outline reasons why a marketing department would engage in market segmentation. (10 marks)

(b) Evaluate three promotional methods for a product or service of your choice. (2002, 30 marks)

Answer

(a) A marketing department would engage in market segmentation for the following reasons.

 (i) If they can segment the market into three or four parts, then they can also identify three or four different target markets which can be approached with different marketing tactics/strategies.

 (ii) The firm can develop different features for the product to meet the specific needs of each market segment and increase its sales as a result.

 (iii) The firm can practise price discrimination, charging different prices to the different market segments. This allows the firm to maximise the revenue it will earn by getting each segment to pay the highest price they are willing to pay.

 (iv) The firm can place advertisements for the product in different media and at different times so as to reach the different market segments with appropriate advertisements.

(b) Promotional methods for Choco Ice Cream Tubs

   (i) Giving out free samples in stores and supermarkets is a very effective way of promoting a food product, as most customers will try the product and can then decide to purchase. This also works because it is close to the point of sale and people are more likely to make a purchase. The person giving out the samples also has the opportunity to tell the customer about the benefits of the product.

   (ii) The firm can run a competition for children, who are the main target market for Choco Ice Cream. If they collect three labels from the packs, they can enter the competition and win one of a number of great prizes. This type of promotion is very effective because most children are attracted to winning a prize and so they will get their parents to buy the product for them so that they can enter the competition. This promotion gets each consumer to buy the product at least three times so that they will get to like the product. The firm can also judge the effectiveness of the promotion from the number of entries received.

   (iii) The firm can offer 50 per cent off coupons for the next purchase of Choco Ice Cream. This encourages the consumer to buy the product because they can get their next purchase for half price. The consumer may also purchase several packs of ice cream in order to have coupons to buy the product cheaply in the future. Again, this method ensures that the consumer uses the product several times so that they grow to like the product.

Practice questions

Higher Level short questions

1. Explain the advantages for a business of adopting the marketing concept. (1999, 10 marks)

2. Identify and chart the stages of the product life cycle. (2001)

3. Outline two channels of distribution. Identify a product which would suit each channel.

Higher Level long questions

1. Describe how a good marketing strategy (plan) would aid business expansion. (2000, 10 marks)

2. Illustrate the importance of the different channels of distribution available to a firm.

3. How might a business decide where to advertise a product? Illustrate your answer with suitable examples.

4. Evaluate the elements of the marketing mix, using a product or service of your choice. (2003, 35 marks)

1.4 Expanding the business

Reasons for business expansion

- Gain control of new products.
- Block competition.
- Diversification.
- Eliminate competition.
- Gain control of new technology.
- Gain control of raw material supplies.
- Increase market share.
- Obtain a dominant position.
- Take advantage of economies of scale.

Study tip

You should be able to list and explain six reasons why businesses expand.

How businesses expand

Organic growth (internal)

This is a gradual growth that is produced from within the firm. Some or all of the firm's profits are reinvested in the business to ensure future growth. Organic growth is achieved by increasing product sales.

Inorganic growth (external)

This type of growth is achieved by joining the firm with another firm or by the takeover of another firm. This results in growth by sudden leaps as a result of mergers, takeovers/acquisitions or joint ventures/strategic alliances.

Study tip

Make sure you can explain and give examples of organic and inorganic growth.

Controls on expansion

The Competition Authority was set up by the government to ensure that consumers and other businesses are protected from unfair practices by market-dominant firms, e.g. charging high prices, restricting supply, exerting pressure on customers or trying to force smaller competitors out of the market.

EU competition policy also ensures that companies do not abuse a dominant position in their market.

Finance for expansion

- Grants.
- Issuing new shares.
- Loans.
- Owner's capital.
- Retained earnings.
- Venture capital.

Study tip

You should be able to discuss the benefits of each type of finance for expansion and make a comparison between any two forms of finance.

Effects of expansion

Business expansion creates changes for:

- Consumers.
- Corporate identity.
- Employees.
- Financial structure.
- Investors.
- Organisational structure.
- Product mix.
- Suppliers.

Study tip

You should be able to discuss the implications of expansion for different aspects of the business.

Make sure you know the following:

- Reasons for expanding a business.
- Sources of finance for expansion.
- The effects of expansion.

Sample exam question and answer

An Applied Business Question (ABQ) is compulsory on the exam each year. The ABQ given below relates to exam years 2006, 2011, 2016 and 2021.

Question

AORA

Aileen O'Rourke established her ladies fashion business and label, AORA, almost three years ago. Aileen had studied design at college and had graduated with distinction, coming among the top 10 per cent in her class. Because of her desire and drive to succeed in anything she undertook, the business developed well. She had the flair and creativity necessary for the enterprise to thrive. Over the past year, however, competition from European designers and manufacturers has been growing. She was beginning to notice delays and shortages that were not a feature of the business in the past. A family friend who was experienced in business management had indicated to her that the controls in her business were not as tight as he would have expected and changes in these areas were essential.

Aileen had a democratic management style. This had worked well up to now, but she was having doubts if the changes needed in the business could be achieved with such a management style. While her advisor has indicated that changes are needed quickly to raise standards and retain customers, he has not pointed out to her how she might go about making the changes.

The business also needs an injection of capital. It needs to expand and acquire the technology to produce the high-quality products for the niche market that the AORA label is aiming at. From her meeting with her advisor, Aileen knows that a credible business plan to guide the future of the business and for presentation to the financial institutions is an immediate requirement.

(a) Illustrate two areas of control that you would recommend to be put in place immediately in the business. Outline one reason in each case and refer to the above text in your response. (30 marks)

(b) Discuss strategies that Aileen could use to successfully manage the change process in the business. Explain your answer fully. (30 marks)

(c) Using appropriate business headings to guide your thinking, describe how you see the future of the enterprise. Make relevant assumptions that you feel may be necessary given the details above. (20 marks)

Answer

(a)

Stock control

The business needs to put a proper stock control system in place because poor stock control can lead to disruption to production due to shortages of materials and loss of orders if the business is out of stock. This is evident in the text: 'She was beginning to notice delays and shortages'.

An effective stock control system should include:
- Computerised stock records.
- Set minimum and maximum stock levels.
- Reorder stock levels and reorder quantities for each item of stock.
- A buffer stock to cover emergencies.
- Regular stocktaking that is reconciled with stock records.

Quality control

The firm needs to introduce a proper quality control system to ensure that customers are always fully satisfied with the quality of the products they are buying from the firm. This will ensure customer loyalty in the face of competition. The need for quality control is indicated in the text: 'her advisor has indicated that changes are needed quickly to raise standards and retain customers'.

An effective quality control system should include:
- Routine testing of raw materials and finished product quality.
- Taking part in a quality certification scheme such as ISO 9000 to assure customers about quality.
- Setting up staff quality circles to discuss improvements to quality.
- Development of a total quality management system within the business.

(b) There are a number of strategies that Aileen could use to successfully manage the change process in the business.

1. She could use a facilitator approach to management, which encourages staff to take on responsibility with advice, support, training and resources provided by her. Staff will then be able and willing to respond to the changes which face the business.

2. She should also empower her key staff to take on the role of decision making in carrying out their responsibilities. The staff will then be able to act when they know it is necessary because they have the power to do so from their manager. Again, this will ensure action is taken where needed in response to change.

3. A teamwork approach can also make staff more responsive to change. Effective teams working on projects are likely to see and work out solutions to problems presented by changes in the business.

4. The firm should learn about and use new technologies quickly rather than ignoring these changes and allowing other firms to gain competitive advantage: '*It needs to expand and acquire the technology to produce the high-quality products.*'

5. Training needs to be continuous to provide staff with better skills and also a wider range of skills so that they can take on different and more complex tasks demanded by changing situations, e.g. using new technology and operating control systems.

6. The firm could implement a total quality management (TQM) approach, which continuously seeks to make improvements to how the business operates in responding to the changing needs of customers. This TQM focus makes the firm better able to react well to changing circumstances and take advantage of them.

(c) The future of the business should be very positive provided the correct action is taken in the following areas.

- Planning: With a lot of change ahead, Aileen needs to ensure that detailed plans are made to guide the successful completion of each project. Regular reviews will allow her to see the need for adjustment to each plan as time goes on. Good planning will allow the firm to be proactive in anticipating change and to manage change better in the future.

- Technology: The efficient introduction of new production technology is clearly going to be a key element in the success of the firm and will enable it to produce 'the high-quality products for the niche market'. It will be very important that staff are fully trained to operate the new technology to get the most advantage from it. Other technological change may need to be introduced to improve marketing and communications in the firm.

- Competition: The firm should be able to withstand the competitive pressures from European firms by firstly introducing quality control systems that ensure the highest-quality products. The new production technology should ensure quality products and should also provide cost savings, which will allow the firm to compete better on price. Aileen has 'the flair and creativity necessary for the enterprise to thrive.'

- Expansion: Aileen should carefully assess whether expansion is possible at present given the level of competition from 'European designers and manufacturers'. Market research is needed to confirm opportunities for expansion and a detailed business plan needs to be produced to support the expansion. Expansion to a bigger scale of production might allow the firm to reduce its costs through economies of scale and as a result compete successfully and increase its sales significantly. The business plan will also be needed to convince investors, shareholders or banks to risk investing more money in the firm.

- Management approach: Aileen needs to make a definite decision about what management style she will adopt for the future. Her own inclination is towards the democratic style and it would also seem suitable to the type of business she is in. A further move towards the facilitator approach to management will help the firm adapt to change more effectively in the future. It would not make sense to dramatically change her management approach to an autocratic style.

Practice questions

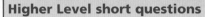

Higher Level short questions

1. Identify two reasons why organic growth may be better for a firm than inorganic growth.

2. Explain what is meant by a strategic alliance and give one example to illustrate your answer.

Higher Level long questions

1. Outline how a business might grow organically. In your opinion, is this the best way for a business to grow?

2. In what ways might the expansion of a business affect (a) employees (b) consumers (c) profits?

3. A business is planning to expand by introducing a range of new products. Evaluate three long-term sources of finance suitable for this planned expansion.
   Paula and Thomas have recently returned to Ireland having worked with transnational companies for ten years. They wish to set up in business together in Ireland manufacturing a range of new organic breakfast cereals. Paula has particular expertise in production and finance and Thomas in marketing and human resources.

4. In time, Paula and Thomas intend to expand the business into the EU market.
   (i) Describe the implications for the business of expansion.
   (ii) Explain two methods of expansion you would advise them to consider. (2006, 20 marks)

2007 Business in Action questions

1. Explain four pricing policies that businesses can adopt as part of their marketing strategy and apply one of them to a product of your choice. (30 marks)

   (i) What is a marketing plan?
   (ii) Evaluate the role such a plan can have for a business. (20 marks)

   Outline and illustrate the term 'niche market'. (10 marks)

CHAPTER 6
The domestic business environment

●●● Learning Objectives

In this chapter you will learn about:
1. Categories of industry.
2. Ownership structures.
3. Community development.
4. Business, government and the economy.
5. Ethics and social responsibility in business.

6.1 Categories of industry

Four factors of production

In producing any product, a business requires four different elements or factors to be brought together to allow production to take place: land, labour, capital and enterprise.

Categories of industry

- Primary sector: Extractive industries.
- Secondary sector: Construction and manufacturing industries.
- Tertiary sector: Service industries.

Primary sector: Extractive industries

The main industries in this sector in Ireland are agriculture, fishing, forestry and mining and quarrying. These industries are built on the natural resources of the country.

Study tip

REVISE WISE
STUDY TIPS

You should be able to describe the main primary industries and to evaluate the importance of these industries to the economy.

Secondary sector: Construction and manufacturing

Construction

The construction industry is important because it uses a high percentage of home-produced raw materials and provides high levels of employment because it is labour intensive. Most construction companies are indigenous, which means profits remain in the country.

Manufacturing

Manufacturing industries take raw materials and convert them into finished goods. The manufacturing sector in Ireland produces food and drink products, pharmaceuticals, chemicals, electronic and computer products.

We devote particular attention to three groupings of manufacturing firms:

- Agribusiness: Firms that either manufacture products for supply to farmers or manufacture finished products based on the output farmers produce.
- Transnational corporations (TNCs): TNCs, also known as multinationals, are companies that have a head office in one country but operate in a number of different countries. For over 40 years, the Industrial Development Authority (IDA) has successfully attracted TNCs to operate in Ireland. There are now over 1,100 foreign-owned companies in Ireland, employing 120,000 people.
- Indigenous firms: Businesses that are Irish owned and involved in production in Ireland. Government policy is to encourage an increase in the number and size of indigenous firms through the state agency, Enterprise Ireland.

Trends in manufacturing:

- World-class manufacturing has grown, particularly due to the presence of large TNCs operating in Ireland. This greatly increases export sales due to high quality standards.
- The level of investment in R&D by manufacturing companies has grown.
- A number of the new TNCs setting up in Ireland have established regional bases with manufacturing, marketing, R&D and customer service all operating from Ireland.
- A growing number of indigenous firms are setting up in the high-technology sector, developing products for world markets in communications and computers.

Study tip

Make sure you can give an outline of the industries involved in the secondary sector and explain their importance to the economy. You should also be able to discuss the role of indigenous firms and TNCs in the economy.

Tertiary sector: Service industries

Ireland has important service industries, such as banking and finance, travel and tourism, design, advertising, transport and distribution, professional services, recreation and leisure, catering and maintenance and repair.

The services area is the fastest-growing sector in Ireland, providing a high percentage of new jobs. More than 60 per cent of the Irish labour force is working in services.

Trends in service industries:
- The demand for services has increased greatly due to increased prosperity.

- There has been an increase in leisure and entertainment services.
- ICT services continue to be developed, such as the use of mobile phones, e-mail, text messaging and broadband services.
- There has been growth in the number of firms operating telecentres.
- Irish firms are now selling services abroad, e.g. education, design, consultancy and financial services.
- There has been rapid growth in child care services in recent years.

Study tip

Make sure you can explain the importance of service industries in the economy.

Key points

Make sure you know the following:
- Primary sector industries.
- Secondary sector industries (construction and manufacturing).
- Tertiary sector industries.

Sample exam question and answer

Question

Using examples, explain the impact of transnational companies in Ireland. (2004, 20 marks)

Answer

Transnational companies have a great impact in Ireland in the following ways:

1. TNCs employ thousands of Irish people directly in a very wide range of disciplines. TNCs are usually large firms and can often employ hundreds of workers in one business. For example, The Pfizer Chemical Corporation employs a very large workforce at Ringaskiddy, County Cork.

2. The local economies close to TNCs receive a big boost from the additional spending by employees. This may result in more people being employed locally, as is the case in Ringaskiddy and surrounding areas.

3. Many new indigenous Irish firms have set up to supply goods and services to TNCs. These firms have grown and have employed additional staff.

4. The Irish government has collected millions of extra euro in taxes as a result of the TNCs operating here, e.g. VAT, PAYE and corporation profits tax.

5. TNCs have provided world-class training and skill development to thousands of Irish workers. These skills have been passed on and shared by other firms that have subsequently employed these workers. In the case of Pfizer, the skills are in chemical production. Many past employees of Pfizer joined other new chemical companies in the Ringaskiddy area and brought their skills and experience with them.

6. Most of the output of TNCs has been exported, contributing greatly to the balance of payments. Output sold in Ireland has mostly replaced imports, thus further improving the balance of payments. Pfizer exports most of its output to their other factories abroad.

7. The output of all the TNCs contributes to gross national product and greatly enhances the standard of living in the country.

8. Sometimes TNCs will close down unexpectedly and move to another location. This has caused great hardship in some areas of Ireland where there was a dependence on one particular TNC.

Practice questions

Higher Level short questions

1. Explain the term 'service industry'. (2003)

2. Illustrate your understanding of the term 'indigenous firm'. (2003)

3. Name and give an example of each of the three types of industry. (2002)

4. What is a transnational company? Name two transnational companies. (1999)

Higher Level long questions

1. (a) Outline the main industries in the primary sector in Ireland.
   (b) Briefly evaluate the benefits of these industries to the country.

2. Evaluate the benefits for Ireland of having a large number of transnational corporations operating here.

3. Discuss the importance of the construction and manufacturing sectors in industry in Ireland.

4. Outline the categories of industry in the Irish economy. In the case of one of these, describe its contribution to the economy. (2006, 20 marks)

5. Discuss the importance of the categories of industry to the current Irish economy. (2007, 20 marks)

6.2 Ownership structures

Sole trader

- A business that is owned and run by one person.
- No formalities except registration of a business name.
- Small businesses often with family involvement.

Benefits:
- Easily set up.
- Few regulations.
- Owner has full control.
- Owner receives all profits.
- Flexible.
- Privacy.

Drawbacks:
- Heavy pressure and workload on owner.
- Owner carries all the risks.
- Shortage of capital.
- Lack of expertise.
- The owner has unlimited liability.

Partnership

- A business owned and run by between two and 20 people in order to make a profit.
- No formalities except registration of a business name.
- A partnership agreement, called a Deed of Partnership, may be drawn up.
- At least one partner must have unlimited liability for the debts of the business.

Benefits:
- Easy, quick and cheap to set up.
- Workload and risks are shared.
- More expertise is available.
- More capital is available.
- Subject to few regulations.

Drawbacks:
- Profits must be shared.
- Partners have unlimited liability.
- Partners may disagree.
- The partnership ends if one partner dies.

Private limited company

- A business that is owned and controlled by a number of shareholders through the purchase of shares in the company.
- Can have up to 50 shareholders. *→ can only lose what they put in*
- Shareholders have limited liability for the debts of the business.
- The company is a separate legal entity from its owners.
- The company can sue and be sued. *in its own name.*

- Capital is invested in the business through the purchase of shares, which represent part-ownership of the business.
- Major decisions are made at an annual general meeting (AGM).
- One share carries one vote at an AGM.
- Shareholders elect a board of directors to run the business.
- Limited companies are regulated by the Companies Acts 1963–99.
- Accounts must be audited annually by an accountant.

Benefits:
- Separate legal entity from the owners/shareholders.
- Limited liability encourages shareholders to invest.
- More scope to raise capital by issuing shares.
- Banks are more willing to lend to limited companies.
- Shares can be inherited when a shareholder dies.

Drawbacks
- Many formalities and costs in setting up a limited company.
- Subject to many laws and regulations.
- Annual returns must be sent to the Registrar of Companies.
- Shares cannot be sold freely by shareholders.

Public limited company

- A public limited company (PLC) is one whose shares can be freely bought and sold by the public on the stock exchange.
- There are at least seven shareholders, with no maximum limit.
- PLCs are highly regulated under the law and by the rules of the stock exchange.
- Annual returns, including accounts, must be sent to the Registrar of Companies.

Benefits:
- Can raise finance for expansion through the issue of shares.
- Shareholders have limited liability.
- High-profile image and publicity.
- Good credit status with banks.
- Can attract top managers.
- Shares or share options can be used to reward and motivate staff.
- Shares can be used as a form of payment in the takeover of another firm.

Drawbacks:
- Company formation costs can be very high.
- There may be conflict between the shareholders and the board of directors.
- The accounts and other information about the firm must be published each year.
- PLCs are prone to takeover because the shares may be bought up on the stock exchange.

Co-operative societies

A co-operative is a business that is owned and run democratically by at least seven owners who share a common interest, e.g. a producers' co-op involving farmers who all want a market for their milk.

● Co-ops have at least seven members or shareholders.
● An application must be made to the Registrar of Friendly Societies to form a co-op.
● Accounts and other information must be sent to the Registrar of Friendly Societies each year.
● Members put different amounts of capital into the business.
● The members have limited liability for the debts of the business.
● Decisions are made democratically, with each member having one vote regardless of the amount of capital invested.
● A management committee is elected by the members to run the business.

Benefits:
● Members have limited liability.
● All members have equal say in running the business.
● The co-op can expand by getting new members.
● Co-ops have good credit status with banks and can borrow easily.

Drawbacks:
● Expansion is limited to the number of new members the co-op can find.

● Co-ops are highly regulated.
● Annual accounts and other information must be sent to the Registrar of Friendly Societies.
● There may be conflict between the interests of the members and the market situation faced by the management committee.
● Members of the co-op can find it difficult to sell their shares.

State ownership

The government has set up a number of companies, called semi-state bodies or state-sponsored bodies, that are owned, financed and controlled by the state, e.g. the ESB, RTÉ.

● The capital is provided by the government.
● All borrowings are guaranteed by the state.
● The board of directors is appointed by the government.

Study tip

REVISE WISE
STUDY TIPS

You should be able to describe each form of business ownership.
You should also be able to make a contrast between any two named forms of business ownership.

Strategic alliance/joint venture

- This is where two or more firms work together to complete a certain project or to develop a product.
- A separate company may be set up to carry out the joint venture or a legal agreement may be signed.

Benefits:
- Firms can share costs and risks involved in a project.
- Smaller firms can combine to bid for large projects.
- Specialist firms can combine with other firms that have different expertise.
- Marketing alliances with firms abroad can be an effective way to sell products to foreign markets.

Drawbacks:
- Each firm lacks full control over the project.
- Serious disagreement can end the project, with loss of money to both firms.

Franchises

- Under a franchise, a company that owns an established branded product or service allows another firm to produce and/or sell the product in return for a fee.
- A legal contract is drawn up between the franchiser and the franchisee.
- Strict controls apply to how the franchise is operated.
- The franchiser provides advertising and marketing support to the franchisee.
- The franchisee invests capital in developing the franchise.

Benefits:

- Owners of the franchise can expand their business with minimal risk.
- The franchiser can retain control over how the product is marketed.
- The franchisee can start a new business with a proven record of success.
- Consumers benefit from high product standards in outlets worldwide.

Drawbacks:

- Franchisees are limited in what they can do in the business by the franchise agreement.
- All units of the business are affected by any bad publicity.
- The business may lack a personal touch with customers.

Study tip

Make sure you can explain the differences between strategic alliances and franchises as forms of business organisation.

Changes in ownership structure

Reasons for changing from a sole trader to a partnership business:

- To get additional capital from partners.
- The workload can be spread out among the partners.
- New skills and expertise may come with partners.
- Risks are shared by the partners.

Reasons for changing from a sole trader to a private limited company:

- As shareholders, the owners get limited liability for the debts of the business.
- Up to 50 shareholders can contribute capital for expansion.
- New shareholders may bring new expertise to the firm.
- Banks are more willing to lend to limited companies than sole traders.
- A limited company can carry on even if a shareholder dies.

Reasons for changing from a co-operative to a public limited company:

- A PLC can raise unlimited additional capital by issuing new shares.
- PLC status improves the image of the firm, both at home and internationally.
- Takeovers of other firms can be paid for through the issue of shares.
- Original investors in the co-op can sell their shares much more easily.

Changing trends in business ownership structures

- Many new private limited companies have been formed by entrepreneurs who want to limit their financial risks in starting a business.

- Fast-growing companies with global potential for growth have moved to become public limited companies to enable them to finance rapid expansion.
- Many new businesses are setting up under franchise arrangements.
- Many strategic alliances are being formed, some between Irish and foreign firms and some public-private partnerships between the government and private companies.

- A number of large agricultural co-operatives have become public limited companies in recent years, e.g. Donegal Creameries plc.
- The government has also sold a number of state-owned businesses into private ownership, e.g. Telecom Éireann and ICC Bank.

Study tip

You should be able to discuss the reasons why a business might change from one form of ownership structure to another.

Key points

Make sure you know the following:
- Be able to compare the different ownership structures.
- Be able to distinguish between franchises and strategic alliances.
- Know the reasons for changing ownership structure.

Sample exam question and answer

Question

Describe two reasons why a business enterprise might change its ownership structure over time. Use illustrations to support your answer. (20 marks)

Answer

A business enterprise might change its ownership structure over time for the following reasons.

Expansion
If a business is growing fast, it may need to change structure to facilitate the growth of the firm. For example, if the business is a sole trader, it could raise more capital by becoming a limited company and selling shares to new shareholders. It would also be able to attract people with expertise that is required by the business.

Risk

The owners of sole traders and partnerships are exposed to commercial risks and might change the ownership structure to protect themselves from some of this risk. By changing to a limited company, the owners can get limited liability protection, which means that they can only lose the amount of money they have invested in the company by buying shares.

Finance

When a business such as a limited company or a co-operative is growing quickly, they cannot finance all their growth through borrowings, as the burden of debt and interest would be too great. They may need to change to a public limited company, through which they can raise the large amount of interest-free capital that they need.

Privatisation

State-owned companies may be sold by the government because the government believes their future success and profitability will be better in private ownership. Private owners may be able to take a more radical approach to cutting costs to ensure survival. As a PLC, a firm may be better able to raise the finance needed for capital investment. The government has said that it will privatise Aer Lingus for these reasons.

Marketing opportunities

A company operating in Ireland may enter into a strategic alliance with a French company in a similar business to market the Irish firm's products in Europe. This new arrangement will allow the expansion of the Irish firm into the European market using the expertise and experience of a firm that already knows the market.

Practice questions

Higher Level short questions

1. Differentiate between a strategic alliance and a franchise.

2. (a) Explain what is meant by 'limited liability'.
   (b) Name two forms of business ownership that offer limited liability.

Higher Level long questions

1. Identify the main factors that influence businesses to change their ownership structures over time. Illustrate your answer with relevant examples.

2. Compare alliances with franchises as types of business organisations. (2000, 20 marks)

3. Contrast a private limited company with a public limited company as a form of business organisation. (2001, 20 marks)

6.3 Community development

A community is a group of people who live and work together and who are dependent on one another.

The community development process

Community development is a process whereby local people and organisations come together to do things that will improve the locality as a place to live and work.

Stages in the community development process:

- All individuals and groups in the area should meet to discuss the need for development in the area and agree projects to be considered, e.g. the building of an enterprise centre.
- A development team or committee is appointed to identify and carry out the projects. Sometimes a Community Development Association is formed.
- The projects identified are researched and realistic goals are set.
- An audit is conducted of all the community's resources and assets that may be used to achieve the objectives set.
- One or two specific projects are decided on and the development team starts working to complete the tasks.

- The assistance of state and other agencies is sought, including advice, training and finance.
- Regular meetings are called to inform the general population on progress.

> **Study tip**
>
> Make sure you can outline how the community development process operates.

Benefits of community development

- New social and commercial enterprises are set up in the locality.
- Additional employment is created.
- The skills and experience of the local workforce are improved.
- Local resources are exploited to the benefit of the community.
- Increased incomes in the area will boost the local economy and create new business opportunities.
- The people of the community gain confidence in their ability to do things for themselves and for the community.
- Improvements in the locality attract more people to live in the area.
- The community develops a sense of identity and pride in their own place.

Agencies that can help community development

- Area Partnership Companies.
- City and County Enterprise Boards.
- FÁS.
- LEADER Programmes.

How businesses can help community development

- Provide employment for people in the area.
- Firms spend money locally, which boosts the local economy.
- Firms add to the skills base in the community as workers are trained.

- Spin-off industry: If an important supply item is not readily available to a local company, a new business may be set up in the area to produce and supply that item.
- Local entrepreneurs reinvest in new businesses and jobs.
- The growth of business often attracts improvements in infrastructure that makes the area more attractive to new industries.

Study tip

You should be able to discuss how community development benefits business and also how business benefits community development.

Key points

Make sure you know the following:
- Benefits of community development.
- How businesses can help community development.

Sample exam question and answer

Question

(a) Define community development. (10 marks)

(b) Analyse how local communities and local businesses can benefit from each other's presence in an area. Use an example in each case to illustrate your answer. (2003, 20 marks)

Answer

(a) Community development may be defined as the local people and organisations in an area taking the initiative to increase the level of social and economic activity within the community so that the community can thrive and be an attractive place in which to work and live.

(b) Local communities can benefit from a business in the area in a number of ways.

Employment
The business will employ a number of staff directly and most of them will be drawn from the local community. It is important that there are good levels of employment if a community is going to prosper. For example, Tara Mines outside Navan in County Meath provides hundreds of jobs for people living in the community.

Infrastructure
The businesses in an area will attract the necessary infrastructure development from the government to allow the firms to trade successfully, and the local community benefits from this infrastructure. In the case of Tara Mines, they have very good roads and a rail line serving their factory. This is of great benefit to the community and helps in attracting further industry to the town.

Businesses can benefit from the local community in a number of ways.

Employees
The business needs a supply of suitably skilled workers to operate its plant and relies upon the population of the local area for its needs. Workers who live locally are more likely to be on time and to be loyal to their local employer. In Navan, there is a tradition of mining in recent years and the local workers know what is involved in the business. A firm like Tara Mines benefits greatly from the workforce in the local area.

Goodwill
The local population is very important to local business in its goodwill towards the operation of the firm. It is hard to run a business without causing some discomfort to the neighbouring community, whether through traffic, noise or pollution. The business will appreciate the community making allowances for some discomfort caused by the firm and will try to minimise any problems.

Practice questions

Higher Level short questions

1. Identify four positive effects of community development.

2. List three challenges faced by community development organisations.

Higher Level long questions

1. Evaluate the importance of local businesses to a community.

2. Outline the benefits of a community development programme in an area of high unemployment.

3. Discuss how the services provided by one community development organisation in your locality help business enterprises. (2001, 20 marks)

6.4 Business, government and the economy

How the government intervenes in the economy

- Legislation: By passing laws, e.g. the Consumer Information Act.
- Government department decisions.
- Local authority actions.
- Semi-state bodies.

The role of government in the economy:

- Enforces legislation.
- Environmental protection.
- Infrastructure development.
- Provision of services.
- Redistribution of wealth.
- Regional development.
- Regulation.

The effects of government actions on business

- Taxation policy: Some taxes have the effect of creating work and expense for firms, such as collecting PAYE and VAT taxes for the state. Other taxes boost business investment and profits, such as low rates of corporation profits tax.
- Spending policy: When the government increases spending, this creates extra demand for goods and services, which firms can benefit from.
- Government as employer: As the biggest employer in the country, the wages paid by the state to its employees influence the rates of pay that private businesses will have to pay to their workers.

- Decentralisation: Moving government offices out of Dublin to rural locations will provide opportunities for businesses in those local areas.
- Infrastructure: Most of the infrastructure used by business is provided by the government.
- Government planning: Business benefits from the publication of government plans, whether they present opportunities or challenges.
- National agreements: The negotiation of national agreements gives business the opportunity to influence the future direction of the economy.
- Public-private partnerships: These arrangements for the provision of infrastructural projects give new opportunities for private firms to build and manage major projects in partnership with the state.
- Regional development: Businesses in less-developed regions benefit when the state takes action to increase economic activity in those regions.
- Industry grants: The government provides grants to businesses for capital investment, for training of staff and for feasibility studies through a number of different agencies.

Study tip

You should be able to describe how the government can create a favourable climate for business.

State-sponsored bodies/ semi-state bodies

These are organisations that are set up, financed by and are in the control of the state.

Reasons for state involvement in commercial enterprises:
- Develop the country's natural resources.
- Provide essential services.
- Develop the country's infrastructure.
- Have control of strategic industries.
- Develop industries requiring high capital investment.

Important state agencies in Irish business
- Bord Bia.
- CIÉ.
- Enterprise Ireland.
- Environmental Protection Agency.
- ESB.
- Fáilte Ireland.
- FÁS.
- Health and Safety Authority.
- Industrial Development Authority (IDA).
- Labour Relations Commission and the Labour Court.
- RTÉ.

Study tip

Ensure that you can refer to examples of state-sponsored bodies and their role in the economy.

Privatisation of semi-state bodies

Semi-state bodies are sometimes sold into private ownership by the government.

Reasons for privatisation:
- The state may wish to sell a valuable business for cash so that they can use the money in another way.
- The original reasons for owning the business no longer apply.
- Private owners may be better able to make the firm more efficient and competitive.
- State-owned monopolies must be opened up to competition, i.e. deregulated, under EU regulations.
- The firm may require capital investment that private owners would be willing to invest.

- The state may wish to promote investment in shares among the general public.

Economic variables and their effects on business

- Inflation: Wage demands, reduced exports, reduced demand and price increases.
- Taxation: Increased costs, disincentive to invest, increased labour costs and reduced demand.
- Interest rates (higher): Increased costs, fall in demand and less investment.
- Exchange rates: Exchange risk, changes in import and export prices.
- Employment levels (rising): Increased sales, wage increases and increased output.

Study tip

Make sure that you can describe the main economic variables and how they affect business.

Key points

Make sure you know the following:
- The effects of the government on business and the economy.
- The importance of semi-state bodies.
- Reasons for privatisation.
- Economic variables.

Sample exam question and answer

Question

Analyse how the economic variables (factors) in the Irish economy have an impact on business. (1999, 25 marks)

Answer

The economic variables in the Irish economy impact on business in the following ways.

Interest rates

If the cost of borrowing is high, then businesses will have higher costs in servicing their loans. Firms will also be slower to invest in expansion if they have to borrow the finance needed at high rates of interest. High interest rates will also seriously affect consumers' willingness to borrow money to make expensive purchases such as holidays and cars and the overall demand for goods and services will go down in the economy, with adverse effects on businesses generally.

Inflation

If the level of prices is rising quickly due to high levels of inflation, this will affect business. Firms will have to pay higher prices for raw materials and other inputs, increasing their costs and causing them to increase their selling prices. If they cannot increase their prices due to foreign competition, they will have a serious reduction in their profit levels due to the added costs. Inflation also reduces the purchasing power of consumers. As a result, workers will demand increases in wages from their employers. If wage increases are granted to workers, then employers will have to increase their selling prices further, thus adding to the inflationary spiral.

Exchange rates

Exchange rates affect businesses that either buy or sell goods with countries that have different currencies. Firstly, if the exchange rate fluctuates a lot, it creates a high level of uncertainty for the business as it can gain or lose a lot of money depending on whether the exchange rate has risen or fallen. If the value of the home currency rises, then the firm will be able to buy in goods more cheaply, thus reducing costs and increasing profits. A business may switch its purchasing from one country to another because of changes in the exchange rates with those countries.

Taxation

If taxes on business are increased by government, firms will clearly earn less profits after tax. This may affect the ability of firms to invest in future expansion. Higher tax rates may also cause some firms to locate their business in another country which has lower rates of tax on business. Higher rates of tax on consumers reduce their disposable income, and as a result the overall demand for goods and services decreases. This fall in demand will affect the level of sales of firms and their profits.

Unemployment

If there are high levels of unemployment, there will be downward pressure on the rates of pay that firms will have to pay. This will allow firms to reduce their costs and increase their profitability. Firms will also benefit from having many well-qualified and skilled applicants looking for positions with them. However, if the economic variables move in the opposite direction, then the opposite effect would result.

Practice questions

Higher Level short questions

1. Outline two ways by which government helps business.

2. Identify three purposes of government intervention in the economy and give an example of each.

3. List four reasons why the government would set up a semi-state company.

Higher Level long questions

1. Analyse the way in which the government creates a suitable climate for business enterprises in the country. Use examples in your analysis. (2000, 25 marks)

2. Evaluate the arguments for the privatisation of commercial state enterprises.

3. Analyse how the economic variables (factors) in the Irish economy have an impact on a local economy. (2001, 20 marks)

6.5 Ethics and social responsibility in business

Study tip

Make sure you can define what ethical behaviour is and identify the features of an ethical business.

REVISE WISE STUDY TIPS

Ethics in business

Ethics are a set of principles which help an individual or organisation to decide what is right and what is wrong. Firms should do what is morally right and should be honest and fair in their dealings with others.

Features of an ethical business:

- Ethos: The firm sets out its intention to be ethical in its mission statement and all staff understand this.
- Leadership: Ethical behaviour comes from the top down.
- Accountability: Individuals are made accountable for any unethical behaviour and the firm will not seek to protect them from any consequences that arise.
- Whistle-blowing: Staff are encouraged to report any unethical behaviour they come across.
- Code of ethics: The firm adopts a written set of rules to ensure ethical behaviour.
- Training: Staff learn that they must behave ethically on behalf of the firm when they do induction training.
- Ethical audits: Regular checks are done to ensure that the firm is in fact operating in an ethical way.

Social responsibility in business

Firms must take responsibility to look after the interests of all the stakeholders in the business as well as the local community and the society in which it operates. Businesses must be socially responsible to investors, workers, suppliers, customers, the community, the government and society as a whole.

A business can become more socially responsible by:

- Making social responsibility an objective of the firm.
- Consulting widely with all stakeholders about developments in the business.
- Conducting social audits to confirm that the firm is acting in a socially responsible fashion.
- Committing resources towards supporting charitable and community projects.
- Making public commitments to being socially responsible and using this as a positive public relations exercise.
- Making social responsibility a factor in all business decisions.

Environmental issues facing business

- Pollution of air, water and land.
- Climate change resulting from excessive emissions.
- Illegal dumping of waste.
- Unnecessary packaging on products, causing waste.
- Non-renewable resources are being exhausted.
- Renewable resources need to be developed, particularly in the area of energy.
- Environmental legislation is getting stronger and more demanding on business.
- Firms must engage in sustainable development, i.e. the actions of the firm must not have a negative effect on our ability to produce in the future.
- Waste reduction and recycling.
- The polluter pays principle says that a firm or individual can be made to pay for the cost of repairing damage done by pollution.
- Environmental groups, e.g. Greenpeace and Earthwatch, are very active and will lobby to prevent developments if they believe they are bad for the environment.

Study tip

REVISE WISE STUDY TIPS

You should be able to identify the environmental issues facing businesses and the effects of these issues on the operation of the firm.

Features of an environmentally friendly business:

- Consults with stakeholders and environmental groups before embarking on new projects.
- Always carries out an environmental impact assessment (EIA) for any new project to assess its likely impact on the environment.
- Develops a positive ethos within the firm towards the environment.
- Considers the effect on the environment of all decisions it makes.
- Carries out environmental audits on a regular basis to ensure that the firm is not causing damage to the environment.

Cost/benefit analysis of being socially responsible

Costs:
- Higher wage costs to provide employees with fair wages.
- Lower profitability resulting from fairer pricing of products.
- Higher costs of setting up production to minimise pollution.
- Increased R&D costs to develop low-pollution production methods.

Benefits:
- Development of a loyal customer base.

- Having an ethical ethos may reduce theft from the firm by the staff.
- Social responsibility can be a positive marketing point.

- Cost savings through waste reduction and production efficiency.
- Costs to society, e.g. pollution, are greatly reduced.

Key points

Make sure you know the following:
- Features of an ethical business.
- Environmental issues facing businesses.

Sample exam question and answer

An Applied Business Question (ABQ) is compulsory on the exam each year. This ABQ relates to exam years 2007, 2012, 2017 and 2022.

Question

The Inell brand is well established and well regarded in agricultural circles as the brand of quality when it comes to farm machinery. The growth of the business in Ireland has been good in the 20 years since its foundation by the Murphy brothers, Michael and Patrick. They both had surrounded themselves with the best technically qualified and enterprising employees they could find at every stage of the development of the business. They believed in the empowerment of their employees and giving them the chance to prove themselves at every opportunity.

Several suggestions have been put forward at the monthly management meetings recently about the expansion of the business. Expansion, not only on the home market but also into European and world markets, with new and adapted older products, has been discussed. Michael feels that the risks are too high and that losses may result, but Patrick feels that for the business to survive in the future, it must grow in the long term.

The technology in two of the three manufacturing plants located in Ireland is getting old and will be in need of complete modernisation in the very near future, as it is not up to present-day environmental standards. There have been some minor accidents in the plants resulting in criticisms of the company on its care of the environment being published in the newspapers. Both the founding members recognise that they have responsibilities not only to their shareholders and employees but also to their customers and society in general.

(a) Analyse the importance of good employer-employee relationships in the running of companies such as Inell Limited. Refer to the central role of the human resource department in the process. (30 marks)

(b) Discuss two strategies that Inell Ltd could use to successfully expand the business. Make relevant assumptions that you feel may be necessary, given the details above. (30 marks)

(c) Using appropriate headings to guide your thinking, describe how Inell Ltd could become a more socially responsible business. Refer to the above text in your response. (20 marks)

Answer

(a) Good employer-employee relations are very important to the running of companies like Inell Ltd. The human resource department has the responsibility for ensuring a good relationship between employer and employees.

The HR policy was to employ *'the best technically qualified and enterprising employees'* to work in the business. It is important to give such employees challenging and interesting work so that they will get satisfaction from their work and will be motivated to work hard: *'giving them the chance to prove themselves at every opportunity'*.

The HR department must make sure that the payments and rewards system for employees is good and compares well with other employers so that the staff feel they are valued and wanted by the firm.

Inell Ltd has a policy of staff empowerment – *'they believe in the empowerment of employees'* – which gives employees the feeling of being trusted by the employer and also allows them a level of autonomy in doing their work. This makes the employees much more responsive to the needs of the firm.

Communication and consultation with staff is very important when changes are coming so that staff know what's happening and can have some input into decision making: *'suggestions have been put forward at the monthly management meetings'*. Inell have done this so that staff will feel part of the company and will support decisions that are made about the future.

It is important for employees to feel that their employer is concerned about their health, safety and welfare at work. If the HR department takes these issues seriously, then workers will be reassured and will respect the employer for taking responsibility in these areas.

Other possible answers:
- *Provide for flexible working agreements, flexi-time, job sharing, etc.*
- *Opportunities for promotion.*
- *Staff training and development programmes.*
- *Pleasant work environment and conditions.*
- *Social activities for staff.*
- *Open negotiation with trade unions.*

(b) Franchising

To expand its share of the home market where its products and brand are very well known, Inell should make franchise arrangements with companies in each part of the country who will sell the firm's range of products. Franchising can be very effective in expanding a business, but also has the advantage that it does not involve the firm in major capital expenditure on new premises and staff. This will overcome Michael's concerns *'that the risks are too high'*. The firm has a line of new and adapted old products to bring to the market, which will also have the potential for increased sales through the franchise network. Local franchise companies can develop strong local markets for the products in their parts of the country.

Strategic alliances for export markets

The firm can develop new export markets without large capital investments by forming alliances with companies in each of the new markets who will sell the firm's range of machinery. The alliance company in each country will know the market and will share the cost of investment in developing the market. This method gives the benefit of having a local partner with local knowledge and expertise to work with. The firm can continue to produce its products in Ireland and ship them to the export markets.

(c) Inell Ltd could become a more socially responsible business in the following ways.

Company objectives

The firm can set being socially responsible as an objective that is agreed with all the stakeholders. In all future decisions, social responsibility will be considered before any decision is made. If all staff focus on this objective, then the firm will become more socially responsible in everything it does. For example, in replacing the old equipment, they will ensure that the new plant will have no negative impact on the environment and that it will be safe for employees to operate.

Safe production and safe products

The firm can make safety of its operations the focus of its quality control. This could be part of a total quality management system which would ensure that all aspects of production are reviewed to eliminate any risks to employees or the environment. TQM can also ensure that products are designed to the highest safety standards to protect the customer when operating the firm's farm machinery. Product testing for quality and safety must also be done thoroughly. If the firm can ensure minimum risk to employees, the environment and customers, then it can say that it is socially responsible. This would avoid *'criticisms of the company on its care of the environment being published in the newspapers'*.

Social audits

The firm can introduce regular social audits of its activities with the help of an outside expert to identify areas where improvements can be made. Any problem areas can then be addressed and improved on, whether they relate to safety, environmental, equality or ethical issues. In particular, a social audit should be conducted on any new project that the firm embarks upon, such as the modernisation of the two factories or the expansion into foreign markets.

Ethical standards certification

The firm could apply for a certification of ethical standards, called SA8000, which involves outside inspections of its operations to ensure that it does in fact act ethically. If the firm passes inspection, it can then publicise that it meets the ethical standard. This is a good way for a firm to work towards improving its level of social responsibility using an outside agency to set the standards. This ethical certification is international and will help the firm introduce its products to foreign markets.

Practice questions

Higher Level short questions

1. Illustrate your understanding of ethical behaviour by means of an example.

2. Identify two ways a firm can be more socially responsible.

Higher Level long questions

1. Illustrate how socially responsible business practice is good for a business enterprise. (1999, 15 marks)

2. Illustrate how environmental issues impact on businesses. (2000, 15 marks)

3. Evaluate the costs and benefits of being ethical, environmentally friendly and socially responsible for businesses.

CHAPTER 7

The international business environment

edco business REVISE WISE

●●●Learning Objectives

In this chapter you will learn about:
1. The international trading environment.
2. The European Union.
3. Global business.

7.1 The international trading environment

International trade refers to the buying and selling of goods and services between countries. Ireland is a small open trading economy, meaning that we import and export large quantities of goods and services with few restrictions.

Measuring international trade

A country's trade is usually measured by comparing the flow of money earned from exports with the flow of money that leaves the country to pay for imports. The difference indicates whether there is an overall net inflow (surplus) of money or a net outflow (deficit) resulting from international trade. A country would seek to have a surplus of exports over imports.

Three measures of international trade:
● balance of trade = visible exports – visible imports
● balance of invisible trade = invisible exports – invisible imports
● balance of payments = total exports – total imports

Example

Trading data for 2007 (in millions of euro)

Visible exports	3,420
Invisible exports	1,840
Visible imports	2,880
Invisible imports	2,010

Balance of trade

Visible exports	3,420
Visible imports	−2,880
Surplus	540

Balance of invisible trade

Invisible exports	1,840
Invisible imports	−2,010
Deficit	−170

Balance of payments

Visible exports	3,420	
Invisible exports	+1,840	5,260
Visible imports	2,880	
Invisible imports	+2,010	−4,890
Surplus		370

Study tip

Be able to do the calculations above for international trade from a given set of figures.

The benefits of international trade

To business:

- Large markets.
- Economies of scale.
- Low prices for raw materials and capital goods.
- Quality goods available from different suppliers.

To consumers:

- Low prices.
- More choice.
- Better-quality products.

To the economy:

- Can sell surplus production.
- Specialisation (home firms can specialise in producing what they are good at and export to other countries).
- Employment.
- Higher standards of living.

Study tip

REVISE WISE
STUDY TIPS

Make sure you can evaluate the benefits of international trade.

Protectionism

Sometimes governments try to prevent or limit imports coming into the country in order to allow home industries to stay in business. This is called protectionism. The methods used to stop foreign products from competing are called barriers to trade, such as:

- Import taxes.
- Subsidies.
- Embargoes.
- Quotas.
- Non-tariff barriers.

Trends in international trade

- It has become easier over the years to transport goods around the world, thus allowing the growth of trade.
- The new communications systems make it easier and cheaper to do business across the globe.
- The increase in the number of TNCs has added to the growth in international trade.
- Multinational companies are treating the world as one market and selling their products in the same way across many countries.
- New countries are opening up to the idea of international trade, e.g. the Eastern European countries, China, India and the Pacific Rim countries.
- Over 100 countries have made trade between them much easier through agreements organised by the World Trade Organisation.
- Groups of countries in different parts of the world have got together and made agreements to allow free trade between them, e.g. the European Union and the North American Free Trade Area (NAFTA).
- Deregulation means that governments must eliminate artificial barriers to trade, open up state monopolies to competition from abroad and allow foreign companies to compete for state purchasing contracts.

Study tip

REVISE WISE
STUDY TIPS

You should be able to discuss the trends in international trade and how they impact on Ireland or Irish firms.

The World Trade Organisation

- Set up to promote free trade worldwide by removing barriers to trade.
- Works to eliminate special trading advantages arranged between countries.
- Helps to resolve trading disputes between countries.

- Tries to protect the intellectual property rights of companies that have registered patents for designs and inventions.
- Is trying to get countries and trading blocs to remove subsidies to agricultural products.
- Is trying to promote free trade in services.

Opportunities of international trade for Ireland

- Ireland has an advantage as English is the most common language used in international trade.
- The euro currency is a strong and stable one, which makes foreign trade easier for Irish firms.
- Ireland's 'green' image as an unspoiled and unpolluted country makes it easier to export our food and tourism products.
- Due to Ireland's EU membership, Irish firms have free access to trade with the 24 other member countries of the EU.
- World-class manufacturing: Ireland has a reputation for exporting products of a very high standard.
- There are a number of semi-state bodies in Ireland that are effective in assisting Irish firms to export their products, e.g. Bord Bia (food) and Fáilte Ireland (tourism).

- Many TNCs are attracted to set up in Ireland and they export the majority of their output, thus enhancing Ireland's balance of payments.
- Irish firms can make trading connections with the Irish diaspora that is present in many countries around the world.

Challenges of international trade for Ireland

- It is difficult to compete with manufacturers from many other countries on price and quality.
- It is difficult to compete for exports to Europe because of the high cost of transport compared to other EU countries.
- It is relatively expensive to produce goods in Ireland, which makes it difficult to compete on price with goods from other countries, particularly ones where wage levels are low.
- It can be very difficult to communicate effectively because of cultural and language differences in countries we are trading with.
- Trading with countries with different currencies can be difficult as currency values can fluctuate, causing the cost of goods to change even though the actual price remains the same.
- It can be difficult to get payment for goods from foreign countries, particularly if there

is a dispute of any kind. Taking legal action can be difficult and expensive between countries.

Study tip

Ensure that you can explain the opportunities and challenges of international trade.

Key points

Make sure you know the following:
- How to measure international trade.
- The role of the World Trade Organisation.
- Opportunities and challenges of international trade for Ireland.

Sample exam question and answer

Question

Evaluate the opportunities and challenges for Irish business as a result of engaging in international trade. (1999, 30 marks)

Answer

Irish business has a number of opportunities open to it as a result of engaging in international trade.
- Irish manufacturers can get access to supplies of raw materials from any part of the world. They can find supplies at lower prices or of better quality, which allows them to produce a more competitively priced product.
- Irish firms can access huge world markets with their products by developing export markets.
- International trading allows Irish firms to grow much bigger so that they can reduce their costs through economies of scale. The lowering of costs in this way can make the firm more competitive on price.
- International trading exposes Irish firms to new products and ideas from all over the world. The Irish firms can adapt these ideas into their own operations and improve efficiency and sales as a result.

Irish firms face a number of challenges as a result of engaging in international trade.

- Irish firms can find it hard to compete on price internationally because of the high cost of operating in Ireland.
- Irish firms face difficulties and costs in transporting and distributing their products from Ireland because it is an island on the western edge of the European Union. This may put Irish firms at a disadvantage, particularly when competing with firms from mainland Europe in mainland European markets.
- Irish firms also face a challenge in doing business through different languages and also with people who have different cultural backgrounds. This can lead to communication difficulties and loss of business.
- Getting paid can be difficult for goods supplied to foreign firms if there is not a guaranteed method of payment in place. If firms refuse to pay, it can very difficult to pursue the issue across international boundaries.

Practice questions

Higher Level short questions

1. List four benefits of international trade.

2. Explain protectionism. Illustrate your answer with an example.

3. Identify four barriers to trade.

Higher Level long questions

1. Draw up (a) the balance of trade (b) the balance of invisible trade and (c) the balance of payments from the following figures.
   Imports: visible €520 million; invisible €62 million
   Exports: visible €510 million; invisible €97 million.

2. Discuss the changing nature of the international economy. In your response, include the effect it has on Irish business. (2000, 30 marks)

3. Analyse the significance or otherwise of international trade for Ireland. Refer to the development of trading blocs and transnational companies in your answer. (2001, 30 marks)

7.2 The European Union (EU)

Objectives of the EU

- Maintain peace and stability within Europe.
- Improve standards of living and quality of life.
- Establish common values such as democracy, equality and human rights.
- Strengthen and enlarge the union over time.

Member countries of the EU (as of 2006)

Austria	Lithuania
Belgium	Luxembourg
Cyprus	Malta
Czech Republic	Netherlands
Denmark	Norway
Estonia	Poland
Finland	Portugal
France	Slovakia
Germany	Slovenia
Greece	Spain
Hungary	Sweden
Ireland	United Kingdom
Latvia	

Features of the EU

- A number of sovereign states working towards social, political and economic union.
- The EU is based on a number of international treaties agreed by the member states.
- The EU has its own institutions to run its affairs.

- Pooled sovereignty: Each country gives up some of its sovereign powers to the EU so that the EU can act on behalf of all the states in some instances.
- Each member state contributes money to the EU budget each year.
- The EU develops and operates a series of common policies to achieve the objectives of the union.

Institutions of the EU

The three main institutions are the Commission, the Parliament and the Council of Ministers. These three are interdependent and have roles which require them to co-operate with each other in running the EU. The main institutions must consult with each other and act as a check on the activities of the others.

European Commission

Role:
- Proposes new policies for the EU.
- Implements the new policies passed by the EU.
- Is the executive management body of the EU.
- Is the civil service for the EU.

Structure:
- The commissioners are nominated by the member states.
- The president of the commission is agreed by the member states.

- The Parliament must approve the members of the commission.
- Each commissioner is given a portfolio or area of work.

Functions:
- Gives political leadership within the EU.
- Puts forward proposals for new EU laws.
- Makes sure existing EU laws are obeyed.
- Puts the policies of the EU into practice.
- Manages the spending of the budget.

Powers:
- Brings individuals and organisations to the EU courts.
- Imposes fines on those who don't follow EU regulations.
- Censures states that don't fulfil their obligations under EU law.

European Parliament

Role:
- Represent the citizens of Europe who elected the Parliament.
- Protect the rights of the people of the member states.
- Pass new EU laws in conjunction with the Council of Ministers.
- Ensure that the other institutions use their power in a proper fashion.

Structure:
- Members of the European Parliament are directly elected by the citizens of the member states.

- The Parliament has a large number of committees that deal with different areas of its work.

Functions:
- Discusses proposed new laws.
- Suggests amendments to proposed laws.
- Passes some laws jointly with the Council of Ministers.
- Approves the annual EU budget.
- Monitors how the budget is spent.
- Vets and appoints the members of the Commission.
- Questions the Commission and the Council of Ministers to ensure they are acting properly.

Powers:
- Passes some laws in conjunction with the Council of Ministers.
- Approves the EU budget.
- Appoints and dismisses the Commission.

Council of Ministers

Role:
- Makes all the major decisions of the EU.
- Decides on the future development of the EU.

Structure:
- One minister from each member state sits on the Council of Ministers.
- The Council is sometimes made up of the prime ministers, finance ministers or other ministers from member states.

Functions:
- Sets the objectives for the future.
- Maintains co-operation and trust between the member states.
- Provides leadership for the EU project.

Powers:
- Makes decisions on behalf of the EU, sometimes jointly with the Parliament.

Study tip

You should be able to describe each of the main institutions of the EU and their relationship to each other.

Steps in the EU decision-making process

1. A proposal for a new law is drafted by the Commission and sent to the Parliament.
2. Parliament discusses the proposal and suggests amendments, which are returned to the Commission.
3. The Commission redrafts the proposal and submits it to the Council of Ministers.
4. The Council of Ministers meets to agree or reject the proposal, sometimes as a co-decision with the Parliament.

How interest groups can influence EU decision making

- Lobbying decision makers.
- Setting up offices close to the EU institutions.
- Setting up meetings with individuals and groups within the EU to put their case forward.
- Conducting public relations campaigns.
- Public protest.
- Targeting all those who have input into EU decisions.

Study tip

You should be able to describe the decision-making process of the EU and how interest groups can influence it.

Common policies of the EU

There are a number of areas where the EU has developed common policies to achieve its objectives throughout the member states:
- Single European Market (SEM).
- Economic and Monetary Union.
- Common Agricultural Policy.
- Competition policy.
- Social policy.
- Environmental policies.

Single European Market (SEM)

- A free internal market without barriers or restrictions to trade.
- The free movement of goods, services, capital and labour between the member states.
- Common standards for goods and services in all European markets.
- Recognition of qualifications within all member states.

145

- Common import taxes on goods coming into all member states.
- Government contracts must be open to firms from other member states.

Benefits of the SEM for Ireland:
- Irish firms can sell their products to a very large market.
- Irish firms can expand and achieve lower costs through economies of scale.
- Irish consumers get better choice, quality and price as a result of the single market.
- Transport and distribution costs are reduced with the removal of border checks between countries.
- Ireland can attract non-EU firms to set up here because they can gain access to the single market as a manufacturer based in Ireland.

Drawbacks of the SEM for Ireland:
- Smaller Irish firms may not be able to compete with foreign competitors.
- The government loses the power to protect home industries with tariffs.
- Ireland lacks the large-scale producers that can compete with multinationals.
- The Irish government can no longer give its contracts to Irish firms unless they are the most competitive.

Economic and Monetary Union (EMU)
- A uniform European economy which allows a number of countries to share a common currency, the euro.
- Eurozone countries must meet economic criteria in relation to inflation, interest rates, government spending and national debt.
- The monetary system is run by the European Central Bank (ECB), which issues notes and coins and sets interest rates.

Benefits of the EMU for Ireland:
- Irish firms and individuals do not have to exchange currencies when dealing with Eurozone countries.
- The direct comparison of prices between Eurozone countries puts downward pressure on prices in Ireland.
- Savings are made by not having to pay currency exchange charges to banks.
- Membership of the Eurozone forces the Irish government to maintain economic stability.
- Exchange risks are eliminated when trading within the Eurozone.

Drawbacks of the EMU for Ireland:
- The government loses some control over the economy, e.g. interest rates.
- Our main trading partner, Britain, is not part of the Eurozone.

Common Agricultural Policy (CAP)

- A single market for agricultural products in the EU, with the same prices paid to all producers.
- EU farmers got preference by means of import tariffs on agricultural products from outside countries.
- EU farmers received export refunds to subsidise them when they exported produce onto world markets.
- Excess production is bought, stored and eventually disposed of by the EU, either by destruction or by sale at very low prices on world markets. This is called the intervention system.
- Price supports and direct payments to farmers are funded by the EU budget.
- Grants are available to invest in new technology and to switch to different crops which are not overproduced.
- Overproduction is now discouraged by production quotas and levies.
- Farmers are paid not to produce those crops where there is overproduction.

Benefits of the CAP for Ireland:

- Irish farmers have received huge amounts in financial support through the intervention system.
- Irish farms have been able to modernise and become more efficient with grants from the CAP for investment in technology.
- The Irish economy has benefited greatly from the financial support of the CAP, as agriculture is an important industry.
- Food production has been assured, even if this is at a high cost to the EU.

Drawbacks of the CAP for Ireland:

- Guaranteed markets and prices have led to an over-reliance on a few agricultural products such as milk and beef.
- Mechanisation and bigger farms have reduced the numbers employed on the land.
- Overproduction has led to excessive use of chemicals and problems with agricultural pollution.
- The CAP caused Irish farmers to become dependent on price and market supports.
- Ongoing reform to reduce spending on the CAP is adversely affecting farm incomes.

EU competition policy

- Have free and open competition for all goods and services within the EU.
- Pursue the progressive removal of all barriers to open competition.
- Outlaw the abuse of a dominant position by large firms.
- Ban the operation of cartels, where firms collude to manipulate a market.
- Examine all proposals for mergers of firms to ensure that they do not create new dominant firms in markets.

- Remove all monopolies, both private or state owned, so that competitors can enter the market.
- Public procurement contracts must be transparent and must be awarded to the best bidder.

Benefits of competition policy for Ireland:

- Increased competition gives consumers better choice, quality and price for goods and services.
- It is easier for new, smaller firms to set up and compete in the market, which benefits smaller-scale firms in Ireland.
- The power of inefficient and high-priced monopolies is reduced.
- State monopolies are eliminated and consumers have a choice of supplier.
- Regulation of mergers and takeovers prevents new monopolies from being created.
- Market manipulation by dominant firms is reduced.

Drawbacks of competition policy for Ireland:

- Open competition can result in the closure of many small firms and in the domination of the market by a few multinational firms.
- Closures due to competition can result in unemployment in some industries.

- Free competition may mean that services will not be provided in less profitable sections of the market that were previously provided by monopolies as part of their social role.

EU environmental policies

- Promotion of more environmentally friendly forms of power.
- Grant aid for the development of new technologies which benefit the environment.
- The 'polluter pays' principle ensures that those found responsible for pollution bear the cost of the clean-up.
- Future economic development must be sustainable in its impact on the environment.
- All EU-funded projects must pass an environmental impact evaluation.
- Green taxes should be introduced by governments to promote decisions which are favourable to the environment.
- Promote the development of more energy-efficient public transport systems.
- Require all developments to have an environmental impact assessment carried out before the project goes ahead.

Benefits of environmental policy for Ireland:

- EU funding for environmentally beneficial developments.

- An increased awareness of the need to protect the environment.

Drawbacks of environmental policy for Ireland:
- There are increased costs associated with the protection of the environment.

Benefits to Ireland of EU membership

- Free access to a large market.
- Attraction of foreign direct investment.
- A strong international currency, the euro.
- Financial supports to agriculture.
- Grant aid for the development of infrastructure.
- Economic growth and better control of the economy.
- Better protection of the environment.
- Better rights for workers, consumers and individuals.
- Improved standards of living.

Study tip

Make sure you can outline the main common policies of the EU and the effect of each one on Ireland.

Key points

Make sure you know the following:
- Institutions and decision-making process of the EU.
- EU common policies.
- Benefits of EU membership for Ireland.

Sample exam question and answer
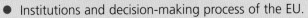

Question

Evaluate the significance of the Single European Market for Irish business.

Answer
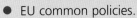

The Single European Market has had significant effects on Irish business in the following ways.
1. Free access to the whole of the European market has allowed Irish firms to greatly increase their sales of goods and services by developing their export markets.

2. Operating in such a large market has allowed many Irish firms to grow large enough to benefit from economies of scale. This has allowed them to reduce their costs of production and to be more competitive on price in the market.

3. The existence of the single market has allowed the Irish government to attract many firms from outside the EU to set up in Ireland. These firms get access to the very big market in the EU without having to pay any import taxes. The arrival of these transnational corporations has greatly strengthened Irish business and brought increased employment and wealth.

4. With the free movement of labour, Irish firms have been able to employ workers from other EU countries at lower pay rates than Irish workers. This has reduced costs for Irish firms and allowed them to become more competitive. Irish firms have also been able to overcome shortages of skilled labour by employing workers from other EU countries.

5. Over the years, Irish business has developed a number of new markets in different EU countries as a result of the Single European Market. This has widened our markets and made Irish business less dependent on our main traditional export market, the United Kingdom.

6. The Single European Market has brought a lot of foreign competition into the Irish home market, forcing Irish firms to reduce their prices and lower their profits and also to improve the quality of their products.

7. Some traditional Irish manufacturers have closed down because they could not compete with the very big competitors from European countries.

Practice questions

Higher Level short questions

1. Name the three main institutions of the EU.

2. Complete this sentence: 'The Single European Market helps business because it . . . .' (2001, 10 marks)

Higher Level long questions

1. Explain the decision-making process of the European Union. Include the relevant institutions in your answer. (2001, 25 marks)

2. Outline the purpose of the European Union's competition policy. (2000, 10 marks)

3. Explain the importance for Ireland of: (a) any one of the policies of the European Union (b) any one of the institutions of the European Union. (1999, 30 marks)

4. (i) Outline the decision-making process of the European Union.
   (ii) Explain the term 'EU directive' and the effect of one of them on Irish business. (2006, 25 marks)

   Evaluate the impact on Ireland of any two of the following:
   (i) The Common Agricultural Policy.
   (ii) The Competition Policy.
   (iii) The European Union Social Charter. (2006, 20 marks)

5. Outline, using an example, the role of 'interest groups' in the European Union. (2007, 10 marks)

7.3 Global business

Features of global businesses

- Global marketing: The product is marketed in the same way worldwide, using the same brand and marketing mix.
- Global brands: Brands are developed for a global market.
- Standardised products: The same product is produced and sold globally.
- Production sharing: Different parts of a product may be produced in factories in different countries and assembled at one location.
- Technology: The most up-to-date production and communications methods are employed.

Reasons for the growth of global firms

- Economies of scale: Firms can reduce their costs of operation as a result of increases in size.
- Communications networks: Worldwide communications networks allow firms to co-ordinate their business activities across the world and to market their products on a global basis.
- Transport systems: The development of world transport systems enables firms to ship their products to different parts of the world quickly and cheaply.

- Manufacturing technologies: These allow firms to locate production of their standardised products anywhere in the world at high-quality standards.
- Free trade: The reduction of trade barriers throughout the world has made global operations much easier for firms.
- Need to survive: Growing to the point where the business can operate globally makes it very difficult for other firms to launch takeover bids.
- Global ICT: ICT infrastructure makes it possible for firms to manage and control operations in many parts of the world based on up-to-the-minute information.

Stages in the development of a global business

1. Indigenous firm produces and sells on the home market.
2. International firm produces and exports to a number of foreign markets.
3. Transnational corporation produces products in a number of countries and sells in a number of countries.
4. Global company produces standardised products in a number of countries and markets a standardised product on a global basis.

The global marketing mix

The global firm will develop a standardised global marketing mix that it will apply across all world markets.

Product

- A standard product design is produced to suit all markets.
- Unique selling points (USPs) are identified with global appeal.
- Brand name and logo are developed with the world market in mind.
- Packaging design is also aimed at a uniform international market.

Price

Price will be set at different levels in different markets, depending on:

- The profit margins allowed to local distribution companies.
- The transport and distribution costs in that market.
- The level of competition in the market.
- The levels of local taxes.
- The standards of living in different markets.

Place

- Regional production centres may be used to supply different regions of the world.
- Direct export to the customer in another country.
- Exporting to a subsidiary company that will sell the product in a foreign market.
- Exporting goods to an agent in a foreign country who will sell the product there.
- Selling to trading companies that will export or import the product to the destination market.

- Some global firms will distribute their products through international franchise arrangements.

Promotion

- Promotion on a global basis can yield big cost savings through economies of scale.
- Sponsorship on a global scale can be very effective, e.g. the Olympic Games.
- Advertising and other promotional activities may need to be adapted to the language and culture in various countries.
- Different advertising media may be effective in different markets.
- International trade fairs are used to promote the firm's products worldwide.
- Internet websites in several languages are used to advertise and sell the company's products.
- Public relations activities are utilised on global media.

Study tip

REVISE WISE STUDY TIPS

Make sure you can explain what global marketing is and how a global marketing mix is developed.

Benefits to a firm from operating globally

- Reduced costs from economies of scale, especially in production and marketing.
- Promotional activities can be applied to all markets.
- Production can be located in different countries to minimise the cost of production.
- Latest technologies can be used to maximise efficiency.
- The business can afford to spend on research and development to bring new products forward.
- It can minimise tax paid by manipulating the prices charged between their companies so that they make their profits in low-tax countries.

Key points

Make sure you know the following:
- Features of a global business.
- The global marketing mix.
- Benefits of operating globally.

Sample exam question and answer

An Applied Business Question (ABQ) is compulsory on the exam each year. Below is an ABQ based on Units 5, 6 and 7. This ABQ relates to exam years 2008, 2013, 2018 and 2023.

Question

Cli-He is a new brand name in the children's toys and games business. The name is also that of a new business venture that Clodagh has recently established. An engineering graduate with a flair for design, she has, to her credit, won two innovation awards for product development in recent years. Clodagh sees a bright future for a business with original ideas in the growing children's leisure business. The challenges of setting up a new business venture, however, are very significant, especially where to find the necessary resources and expertise.

Clodagh plans to market the Cli-He brand to a niche segment of the 'green' market. This niche market is made up of environmentally conscious consumers, with high disposable income who have young families. The price of Cli-He products will reflect this environmental premium, but the price range will not be as high as that of competing products.

Clodagh plans that the business will be environmentally conscious in all its production methods and will use raw materials that are sensitive to the environment. Its marketing will make this green image clear to customers. The Irish base for this new business start-up has been agreed with Enterprise Ireland. Future plans include marketing its products into Europe, the US and other parts of the world through the use of the internet. Clodagh feels that online trading is the way of the future and is a suitable way to market her new product range to the target market.

(a) Analyse one short-term and one long-term source of finance suitable for the Cli-He start-up. (30 marks)
(b) Describe how Clodagh can ensure that Cli-He is an environmentally conscious company. (30 marks)
(c) Discuss the challenges facing Cli-He in developing markets abroad. Refer to the above text in your response. (20 marks)

Answer

(a) A short-term source of finance that Cli-He could use for acquiring stock would be trade credit. The firm could buy its supplies of raw materials on credit and negotiate as many credit days as possible from its suppliers. This should allow Clodagh to manufacture and sell finished products and get paid for them before she has to pay her creditors. This is especially important because selling on the Internet does not involve giving credit, and so she should easily be able to finance her stock of materials using trade credit.

A long-term source of finance that Cli-He could use to acquire premises and machinery would be share capital. She would need to find a small number of investors interested in investing in a limited company with an excellent business plan and with an entrepreneur who has already '*won awards for product innovation*'. Long-term equity capital is ideal because it is interest free. However, her fellow investors may also have a say in how the company is run, so she needs to be certain that they can work well together.

(b) Clodagh can ensure that Cli-He is an environmentally conscious company in the following ways:
  1. She should make being environmentally friendly a clear objective of the firm and she should recruit staff with this objective in mind. If staff are selected who have the right attitude to the environment, this objective will be achieved.

2. Clodagh should ensure that all decisions that are made take environmental considerations into account. This will mean that the business plans to be socially responsible and that its activities are environmentally sustainable: '*Clodagh plans that the business will be environmentally conscious.*'

3. Clodagh can show the whole firm from the start that she is conscious of the environment in the way she approaches running the business. If she gives the lead in this way, the rest of the staff will follow her lead.

4. As production engineer and product designer, '*an engineering graduate with a flair for design*', Clodagh can ensure that the production processes have a positive or neutral affect on the environment: '*will be environmentally conscious in all its production methods and will use raw materials that are sensitive to the environment.*'

5. The company can conduct regular environmental audits on its activities. An independent third party should be involved in conducting these audits to ensure an objective view.

6. The firm can be public about its environmentally responsible approach and develop it as a unique selling point for marketing its products successfully to its target market: '*its marketing will make this green image clear to customers.*' Being socially responsible in this way can actually add to the commercial success of the business.

7. Environmental impact assessments should be prepared for all proposed new projects to ensure that they are environmentally sustainable.

(c) Cli-He will face challenges in developing markets abroad:

1. As a small new company with new products, they will face competition in each market from bigger firms with well-established products and market share: '*the price range will not be as high as its competitors' products.*'

2. There will be difficulties with language and cultural differences in developing the European markets, as each country has a different language. It is difficult to communicate your marketing message effectively when you have to translate it into different languages. There is also the possibility that some markets may not accept the product for cultural reasons that we don't understand. A lot of research is needed to overcome these difficulties.

3. The brand name Cli-He is a pun on the Irish word '*cluichi*', meaning games. This will not be easily understood or recognised in foreign markets and will make it difficult for customers to identify with the products.

4. Cli-He is going to market its products through the Internet. This will only be successful if they can design a website that operates in a number of different languages and that presents the products in an attractive way. This is a difficult challenge for the business. While the Internet is successful in selling some products and services, it would be difficult to build a successful business internationally based on Internet sales alone.

Practice questions

Higher Level short questions

1. Identify four features of a business that operates globally.

2. (a) Many transnational corporations have a 'standardised global marketing mix'. What does this mean?
   (b) Name two such companies. (2000, 10 marks)

Higher Level long questions

1. Analyse the reasons for the growth of global businesses.

2. Using examples, explain the importance of global marketing for a global business. (2000, 20 marks)

3. Illustrate the benefits to a firm of operating as a global business.

4. Explain the term 'global marketing' and its role in international business. (2007, 25 marks)

CHAPTER 8

Examination section

Outline of Leaving Certificate Business course

The course is divided into seven units, as follows.

Unit 1: People in Business
- Stakeholders and their relationships.
- Conflicts and how they are resolved.

Unit 2: Enterprise
- Enterprise characteristics and skills.
- The importance of enterprise.

Unit 3: Managing I
- Manager characteristics.
- Management skills and activities.

Unit 4: Managing II
- Household and business finance, insurance and taxation.
- Human resource management.
- Management of change.
- Interpreting accounts.

Unit 5: Business in Action
- Business opportunities.
- Business start-up.
- Marketing.
- Business expansion.

Unit 6: Domestic Environment
- Categories of industry.
- Business ownership structures.
- Community development.
- Government and the economy.
- Social responsibilities of business.

Unit 7: International Environment
- International trading.
- The European Union.
- Global business.

Legislation

Seven pieces of legislation are part of the course:
1. Consumer Information Act 1978.
2. Sale of Goods and Supply of Services Act 1980.
3. Industrial Relations Act 1990.
4. Employment Equality Act 1998.

5. Unfair Dismissals Act 1977–93.
6. Data Protection Act 1988.
7. Company's Act 1990 (Formation of Limited Companies).

Language used in exam questions

The following list of 'outcome' verbs may appear in exam questions at Higher Level.

- Calculate: To find an answer or solution using numerical data and mathematical operations.
- Contrast: To show the differences between things.
- Define: To state the precise meaning of a term or concept.
- Demonstrate: To explain or describe by showing examples, charts, diagrams, graphs.
- Distinguish: To point out the difference(s) between two things.
- Draft: To prepare or draw up a document or letter.
- Explain: To make clear in a detailed manner.
- Identify: To show that you recognise something.
- Illustrate: To make clear by means of examples, diagrams, charts or graphs.
- Interpret: To explain the meaning of something. To make clear or show a particular understanding.
- List: To write down a number of things which have something in common.

- Outline: To give a short summary of the important features of something without going into detail.
- Recognise: To show that you can identify something that you have encountered before.
- Understand: To grasp the meaning of something.

The following 'outcome' verbs appear regularly in Higher Level questions.

- Analyse: To study a problem in detail by breaking it down into its parts and examining possible relationships.
- Apply: To use knowledge or a skill for a particular purpose.
- Compare: To examine two or more things in order to discover their likenesses and differences.
- Differentiate: To distinguish between.
- Discuss: To examine or consider, suggesting a detailed and careful investigation. To debate both sides of an argument.
- Evaluate: To find or determine the worth, value, amount or significance of something. To assess or judge something.

General preparation for the examination

- Familiarise yourself with the examination paper and the types of questions asked.

159

- Do learning revision of business topics each week and make key word summaries.
- Practise past exam questions, always using point form in your answers.
- Practise short questions from past papers, which can be repeated in exams.
- Learn definitions of key business terms (see the glossary in this book).
- Practise calculation-type questions such as ratios, PAYE tax and average clause in insurance (see examples in this book).
- Practise doing Applied Business Questions (see examples in this book).
- Make sure you study the three units of the course that will be examined in the ABQ from your exam year.
- Learn the seven pieces of legislation.
- Make sure you can draw essential diagrams such as a break-even chart, product life cycle, Maslow's Hierarchy of Needs, etc.
- Make sure you understand the 'outcome' verbs (listed above) that are used in examination questions.

Examination paper layout, Higher Level

TOTAL MARKS: 400
TOTAL TIME: 3 HOURS (180 MINUTES)

Section 1
Answer eight out of 10 short questions.   80 marks

Section 2
Applied Business Question (case study).   80 marks

This question is compulsory and has three parts to be answered.

Section 3
You must answer a total of four out of seven questions, as follows:
- One question from Part 1 based on units 1, 6 and 7.
- Two questions from Part 2 based on units 2, 3, 4 and 5.
- One other question from either Part 1 or Part 2.

Four questions @ 60 marks = 240 marks.

The Applied Business Question each year is based on three different units of the course, as follows:
- 2007: Units 4, 5, 6.
- 2008: Units 5, 6, 7.
- 2009: Units 1, 2, 3.
- 2010: Units 2, 3, 4.
- 2011: Units 3, 4, 5.
- 2012: Units 4, 5, 6.

Examination time management

180 minutes for 400 marks.

- Read examination paper and select questions: 10 minutes.
- Section 1: Eight short questions × 4 minutes each = 32 minutes.
- Section 2, Applied Business Question (80 marks): 32 minutes.
- Section 3: Four questions @ 60 marks (24 minutes each) = 96 minutes.
- Read, check and finalise answers: 10 minutes.

Note: Stick rigidly to times for questions.

General examination advice

- Read each question twice and make sure you are clear about what the examiner is looking for in an answer.
- Make a short plan of your answer by noting key words in your answer book, under the heading 'Plan'.
- Always answer in point form, numbering each point you make.
- You should give one point for each five marks earned.

- For each point in your answer
  (1) state the basic point
  (2) explain and develop the point
  (3) illustrate with an example, if possible.
- Identify the question number and section for all parts of your answers.
- Bring your calculator for use in numerical questions.
- Leave some space free after each answer in case you need to add something later on.
- Check that you have answered all parts of all questions.
- Ensure that you answer the required number of questions from each section of the examination paper.

Short questions advice

- Space for answers is limited, so think about your answer and keep it short and clear.
- Learn a short definition of all key terms on the course.
- Learn initials for business terms such as ROI, ATM, EDI and be able to write the full term in words.
- You can answer more than eight short questions if you have time – you will be marked on your best eight answers.

Applied Business Questions advice

- Read the questions you have to answer first before reading the text so that you can identify answers when reading the text.
- Highlight or underline relevant points as you read the text of the ABQ.
- Plan your answer to each part of the question in point form.
- Remember: usually one point is needed to earn five marks.
- Make sure to refer to or quote from the text of the ABQ in your answer, even if not requested to do so.

Section 3 long questions advice

- Answer the required number of questions from Part 1 and Part 2.
- Read the question carefully and ensure you understand what is required in your answer.
- Write a short key word plan for your answer.
- Answer in point form, giving one point for five marks.
- (1) State each point (2) expand or explain it and (3) give an example if possible.

Questions on past Leaving Certificate examination papers

	1999	2000	2001	2002	2003	2004	2005	2006	2007	2008
Unit 1										
People in Business	1AB		1AB		1AB	1A	1AB	1AC		
Consumer Issues			1C	1AB			1C			
Industrial Relations	1C	1ABC		1C		1BC		1B		
Unit 2										
Enterprise					4ABC			4C		
Unit 3										
Management	4A		4B	4B						
Leadership/ Motivation					5		4C	4AB		
Communication	4B	4ABC	4A	4A	5		4C	4AB		
Planning, Organising, Controlling	4C		4C	4C		4AB				

	1999	2000	2001	2002	2003	2004	2005	2006	2007	2008
Unit 4										
Finance for Households/ Businesses	5AC		5A	5AC						
Taxation	5AB		5C	5A						
Insurance	5AB		5B	5AB				5A		
Ratio Analysis	6AB		6AB			6AB		5B		
Human Resource Management					6AC					
Managing Change		5AB C			6B	5AB C				
Unit 5										
Identifying Opportunities	7A	6	7AB	7A	7A	7AB	6ABC			
Getting Started				6AB		2C	5A	6A, 7A		
Marketing	7BC	7B		7BC	7B	7C	7ABC	7BC		
Business Expansion		7AC					5BC	6B		
Unit 6										
Categories of Industry				2A		3B		2A		
Ownership Structures	2A	2B	2A		2A	2BC	2A			
Community Development			2B		2B		2B			
Ethics and Social Responsibility	2B	2A		2B			2C	2C		
Government, Economy and Business	2C	2C	2C	2AB		2A		2B		
Unit 7										
International Trading	3A	3C	3A	3A				3C		
European Union	3B	3B	3B		3AB	3C	3AB	3AB		
Global Business		3A		3B		3AB	3C			

Study Plan

REVISE WISE
STUDY PLAN

Date				
Time				
Section to be revised				

Date				
Time				
Section to be revised				

Date				
Time				
Section to be revised				

Date				
Time				
Section to be revised				

Date				
Time				
Section to be revised				

Date				
Time				
Section to be revised				

Night before exam	
Sections to be revised	

Study Plan

Date			
Time			
Section to be revised			

Date			
Time			
Section to be revised			

Date			
Time			
Section to be revised			

Date			
Time			
Section to be revised			

Date			
Time			
Section to be revised			

Date			
Time			
Section to be revised			

Night before exam	
Sections to be revised	

Study Plan

Date			
Time			
Section to be revised			

Date			
Time			
Section to be revised			

Date			
Time			
Section to be revised			

Date			
Time			
Section to be revised			

Date			
Time			
Section to be revised			

Date			
Time			
Section to be revised			

Night before exam	
Sections to be revised	

Study Plan

Date				
Time				
Section to be revised				

Date				
Time				
Section to be revised				

Date				
Time				
Section to be revised				

Date				
Time				
Section to be revised				

Date				
Time				
Section to be revised				

Date				
Time				
Section to be revised				

Night before exam	
Sections to be revised	

Study Plan

Date

Time

Section to
be revised

Date

Time

Section to
be revised

Date

Time

Section to
be revised

Date

Time

Section to
be revised

Date

Time

Section to
be revised

Date

Time

Section to
be revised

Night before exam

Sections to
be revised

Study Plan

Date			
Time			
Section to be revised			

Date			
Time			
Section to be revised			

Date			
Time			
Section to be revised			

Date			
Time			
Section to be revised			

Date			
Time			
Section to be revised			

Date			
Time			
Section to be revised			

Night before exam	
Sections to be revised	

Study Plan

Date			
Time			
Section to be revised			

Date			
Time			
Section to be revised			

Date			
Time			
Section to be revised			

Date			
Time			
Section to be revised			

Date			
Time			
Section to be revised			

Date			
Time			
Section to be revised			

Night before exam	
Sections to be revised	

Study Plan

Date			
Time			
Section to be revised			

Date			
Time			
Section to be revised			

Date			
Time			
Section to be revised			

Date			
Time			
Section to be revised			

Date			
Time			
Section to be revised			

Date			
Time			
Section to be revised			

Night before exam
Sections to be revised

Study Plan

Date			
Time			
Section to be revised			

Date			
Time			
Section to be revised			

Date			
Time			
Section to be revised			

Date			
Time			
Section to be revised			

Date			
Time			
Section to be revised			

Date			
Time			
Section to be revised			

Night before exam	
Sections to be revised	

Glossary of Terms

Acceptance   Refers to the formation of a contract where the offer of one party to form a contract must be agreed by the other party (acceptance).

Advertising   Communication in written or visual form aimed at consumers to persuade them to buy a product or service.

Agenda   The list of items to be discussed at a meeting.

Agribusiness   Firms involved in supplying agriculture or manufacturing goods based on raw materials from agriculture.

Annual General Meeting (AGM)   A meeting of all the shareholders of a limited company which takes place once a year to make important decisions.

Arbitration   When a third party investigates a dispute between two parties and makes a decision or recommendation to resolve the dispute.

Articles Of Association   A document produced as part of the formation of a company. It sets out the internal rules for the running of the firm.

Autocratic Leader   A leader who keeps tight control on power and directs others using fear of sanctions to motivate staff.

Automated Teller Machine (ATM)   A machine where customers can do their banking when the bank itself is not open. A card and PIN number are used to identify the customer.

Average Clause   Applies in insurance where something is underinsured. Only a proportion (average) of any claim will be paid out.

Balance Of Invisible Trade   A calculation of international trade, which compares income from imports of services with the costs of imports of services.

Balance Of Payments   A calculation of international trade, which compares the income from exports of goods and services with the amount paid for imports of goods and services.

Batch Production   Method of production where a quantity of one product is produced followed by a quantity of a different product using the same production equipment.

Brand Name   A name given to a particular product that allows the consumer to recognise the product, e.g. 7-Up.

Break-Even Chart   A diagram showing the costs and revenues of a firm at different levels of output. It shows the point below which losses are made and above which profits are made, i.e. the break-even point.

Business Plan   A document setting out how a business will operate in the future under a number of specific headings.

Capacity To Contract   An element of a contract that requires that the parties to a contract must have the capacity (ability) to make a legal contract, e.g. be over 18.

Cash Flow Forecast   A plan of cash inflows and outflows which allows a firm to manage its cash and avoid cash shortages in the future.

Caveat Emptor   Literally means 'let the buyer beware'. Consumers should do research before buying to ensure that they will be satisfied with the product.

Certificate Of Incorporation   This document is proof that a new limited company has been formed. It is issued by the Registrar of Companies.

Chain Of Command   A feature of an organisation structure whereby instructions are given from staff/managers at one level to staff at a lower level.

Channels Of Distribution   The various routes which are used to transfer goods from manufacturers to wholesalers, to retailers and finally to consumers.

Code Of Ethics   A set of rules to guide staff in an organisation to ensure that they do the right thing rather than the wrong from a moral point of view.

Collective Bargaining   When groups of employees and employers negotiate pay and conditions in an individual business, in an industry or at national level.

Common Agricultural Policy (CAP)   The EU policy to organise, support and finance the agriculture industry throughout the EU.

Community Development   The process of local people and organisations getting together to do things to improve life in their area.

Competition Authority   A state organisation set up to ensure increased levels of competition in all markets for goods and services in Ireland.

Competition Policy   A set of regulations aimed at ensuring that there is open competition in all markets for goods and services within the EU.

Computer-Aided Design (CAD)   The use of computers and computer software to design products and processes and to produce detailed drawings.

Computer-Integrated Manufacture (CIM)   A manufacturing process which is automated and controlled by computer systems.

Computer-Aided Manufacturing (CAM)   A production system which employs robots to complete repetitive tasks instead of employees.

Conciliation   A third party investigates a dispute and works with the parties to achieve mutual understanding and hopefully a voluntary agreement.

Condition   Part of a legal contract that when broken causes the contract itself to be broken.

Consideration   To have a legally binding contract, each party must give something of value to the other, called a consideration.

Constructive Dismissal   When the behaviour of an employer is such that it makes it impossible for the employee to attend for work.

Consumer   A consumer is someone who buys and uses a good or service.

Contingency Plan   A plan to deal with an unexpected event in the future.

Contribution   A principle of insurance, which states that if a risk is insured twice the two insurers will share the cost of any claim.

Controller Manager   A controller manager runs the business by imposing rules that other staff must follow.

Controlling   A management activity which involves setting targets and monitoring performance regularly so that adjustments can be made to plans to ensure that targets are reached.

Co-Operative Society   A form of business where owners share a common interest and run the business democratically with the benefit of limited liability.

Corporation Profits Tax (CPT)   A tax on the profits earned by a business.

Council of Ministers   The main decision-making institution of the European Union, made up of relevant government ministers from each member state.

Credit Control   Means ensuring that our debtors pay us on time so that we have enough cash to run our business and that no debts remain unpaid.

Creditors   People and organisations that a business owes money to.

Current Account   A working bank account which allows money to be lodged and withdrawn regularly in a variety of different ways.

Current Assets   Things that are of value to a firm which change in value on a daily basis, e.g. stock, debtors, cash.

Current Liabilities   Things that are owed by a firm and which must be paid within one year.

Current Ratio   A measure of the liquidity of a business. Formula = current assets × current liabilities.

Data Protection Act 1988   A law which gives protection to individuals when information about them is stored on a computer.

Data Protection Commissioner   A government office set up to enforce the provisions of the Data Protection Act 1988.

Debenture   A form of long-term loan, usually borrowed from banks.

175

Debt Capital Sources of finance used by a firm which have an annual cost; includes long-term loans and preference share capital.

Debt/Equity Ratio A calculation of the level of indebtedness of a business. It compares the amount of debt capital with the interest-free (equity) capital of the firm.

Delegation When a manager gives a subordinate the authority to carry out certain tasks and makes them responsible for the completion of those tasks.

Deposit Interest Retention Tax (DIRT) A tax on the interest earned by money on deposit. Interest must be collected by the bank and paid to the Revenue Commissioners.

Deregulation Means that governments within the EU must open up state monopolies and allow free competition to be established in those markets.

Desk Research A form of market research where information is collected from existing sources, e.g. books, reports, internet sites.

Directing Occurs when managers give instructions to staff to carry out a specific task in a particular way.

Director of Consumer Affairs Office set up to inform consumers of their rights and to ensure that consumer legislation operates effectively.

Director of Equality Investigations An office set up under the Employment Equality Act 1998 to investigate and resolve complaints of discrimination under the Act.

Dividends Refers to the paying out of some or all of the profits of a firm to the shareholders.

E-Business When a firm uses the internet to do business with another firm.

Economic and Monetary Union (EMU) The EU policy that created a uniform economy across a number of countries which as a result can share a common currency, the euro.

Economies Of Scale Reductions in the costs of running a business which come from operating at higher output levels.

Electronic Data Interchange (EDI) An automated way of carrying out routine transactions between firms using computer technology and software.

Embargo A government ban on the importation of particular goods or all goods from a particular country.

Employee Empowerment Means encouraging employees to make the decisions necessary to carry out the tasks delegated to them as a way of making them take ownership of the tasks to be completed.

Employers' Liability Insurance An insurance to protect employers from claims by employees who suffer injury in the workplace.

Enterprise Ireland A state body set up to promote and support the development of indigenous firms.

Environmental Audit   An assessment of an organisation to establish the impact of its activities on the environment.

Environmental Impact Assessment (EIA)   An examination and report on the potential effects of any new project or development on the environment.

Environmental Policy   A set of EU regulations aimed at ensuring that damage to the environment is minimised and that all development is sustainable.

Ethics   Refers to questions of right and wrong. See also code of ethics.

European Parliament   The EU institution whose members are elected by the people. It represents the people of the EU and seeks to protect their rights in EU legislation.

European Union (EU)   A developing and growing social, economic and political union between 25 European countries.

Eurozone   The 12 countries who currently (2006) have the euro as their currency.

Exchange Rates   The values at which one currency can be exchanged for another in international trading, e.g. €1.00 = $1.18.

Exports   Goods or services produced in Ireland which are sold to other countries.

Facilitator Manager   A manager who encourages staff to take on additional responsibilities and who supports them in doing this with the necessary resources and training.

Feasibility Study   An investigation of a proposed new product to show it can be successfully produced and sold at a profit.

Field Research   A form of market research where data is collected in the marketplace from consumers.

Fiscal Policy   Refers to plans of the government for the collection of taxes and the spending of those tax revenues.

Fixed Assets   Things owned and used by business over a long period of time, e.g. buildings, vehicles, machinery.

Fixed Costs   Set amounts of money that must be paid by a business regardless of the quantity of goods they produce, e.g. the rent for the factory.

Franchise   When one company pays another company a fee to allow them to set up a business using the other firm's business idea and name, e.g. McDonald's.

Free Trade   Refers to countries or groups of countries who buy and sell goods and services with other countries without imposing barriers to trade.

Functional Structure   An organisational arrangement which divides the business into different departments based on the type of work that is done in each, e.g. purchasing department, production department.

Global Business   A very large company which manufactures its products in a number of countries and markets the same standardised products to one global market.

Grants   Monies given to businesses, usually by the government, to help them develop. Grants normally do not have to be repaid.

Green Taxes   Taxes imposed by governments which are intended to influence producers and consumers to behave in ways which are good for the environment, e.g. the tax on plastic bags has greatly reduced plastic bag pollution.

Grievance Procedure   An agreed set of steps that employees and employers must follow if there is an industrial dispute in the workplace.

Gross (Profit) Margin   The gross profit for the year expressed as a percentage of the value of sales for the year. Formula: gross profit/sales × 100 = X %

Gross Profit   The profit earned by a firm in one year from buying and selling goods.

Hire Purchase   A method of financing the purchase of an asset over a period of years by paying instalments. On the last payment the buyer owns the asset, not before.

Household Budget   A plan of the cash inflows and outflows that allows a household to manage its cash and avoid cash shortages in the future.

Human Resources Management   Involves all aspects of dealing with staff on behalf of the company, including recruitment, payment, holidays, staff relations, etc.

Imports   Goods or services bought by Irish firms from other countries.

Indemnity   A principle of insurance that states that the insured person should not be able to make a profit on an insurance claim.

Indigenous Firms   Irish-owned firms operating in Ireland.

Induction Training   Training provided for new employees to help them get to know their job but also the other employees and how the organisation works.

Industrial Relations   Refers to the relationship between employers and employees within a firm.

Industrial Relations Officer (IRO)   A third party appointed by the Labour Relations Commission to assist both sides in an industrial dispute to reach a resolution – this process is called conciliation.

Inflation   Rises in price levels from one year to another.

Information And Communication Technology (ICT)   A range of computer and telecommunications developments which combine to create powerful new tools for business.

Infrastructure   Refers to systems of transport, telecommunications, electricity, gas, airports, sewage, etc. which are developed in a country.

Inorganic Growth   Expansion of a business by joining together with other organisations or by co-operating with external organisations.

Interest Group A group of people who share a common goal or interest and who work together to achieve their objectives.

Interest Rates The cost of borrowing money, usually expressed as a percentage per annum.

International Trade The buying and selling of goods and services between different countries around the world.

Internet The worldwide network of computers through which people and businesses can communicate with each other.

Intrapreneurship When employees within an organisation are enterprising and come up with new ideas.

Investors People or organisations that are willing to provide finance for a business, either by buying shares or by lending money to the business.

Invisible Exports Services sold to foreign markets.

Invisible Imports Services bought from suppliers in other countries.

Irish Congress of Trade Unions (ICTU) An organisation that represents most of the unions in the country and deals with industrial relations issues at a national level.

Issued Share Capital The value of shares that have actually been sold by a company to shareholders.

Job Description Sets out in detail the tasks that have to be done, the duties and responsibilities of the employee and who they will report to.

Job Enlargement Increasing the duties and responsibilities of a person's job to make it more interesting and challenging for them.

Job Enrichment Providing employees with higher levels of responsibility, but also giving them the authority and power to make the decisions that need to be made to carry out their tasks.

Job Production A production system where each item produced is different from every other and must be made separately by specialist staff.

Job Rotation Moving employees to different tasks over time so that they acquire a range of skills and do not become bored with their work.

Joint Venture See Strategic Alliance.

Labour Court This is the 'court of last resort' which investigates and makes recommendations on industrial disputes.

Labour Relations Commission (LRC) A statutory agency that works to improve the industrial relations climate in Ireland. Offers conciliation and arbitration services to resolve disputes.

Leasing A method of financing assets which involves paying on a regular basis for the use of the asset over a set period of time.

Legality Of Form Sometimes a contract must be in a particular form to be a legally binding contract, e.g. an insurance contract must be in writing.

Limited Liability Means that a shareholder in a limited company can only lose the amount of money the shareholder has invested in the business if the firm gets into financial difficulties.

Line Position An employee who takes instructions from a manager above, or who gives instructions to a subordinate below, is in a line position within the organisation.

Liquidity This refers to the cash position of a business or the ability of the firm to pay its short-term debts when they fall due.

Lobbying A range of activities directed at persuading a decision-maker to make a decision which is favourable for your objectives.

Long-Term Finance Funding for a business for a period of more than five years.

Long-Term Liabilities Monies owed by a business that are due for repayment in more than one year.

Manpower Planning Making sure that the firm will have enough staff with the right skills and qualifications for the future needs of the business.

Margin Of Safety The difference between a firm's target output level and its break-even level of output. It shows how much it can fall short of its target and still not lose money.

Market Research The collection of data on the market for a product so that management can make good decisions about the marketing of the product.

Market Segments The total market for a product can be divided into different groups or market segments whose needs as consumers are different from other groups.

Marketing Concept The marketing concept states that a firm should first identify what consumers need and then develop products to meet those needs.

Marketing Mix These are the four main elements of a marketing effort to sell a product successfully, namely the product design, the pricing of the product, the place through which it will be sold and the promotion for the product (4 Ps of marketing).

Maslow's Hierarchy of Needs A theory of motivation that managers can use which is based on satisfying the needs of the employee as a way of motivating them to work hard.

Mass Production A system of production that is highly automated to produce large quantities of product at low cost.

Matrix Structure An organisational structure which allows the formation of teams drawn from different departments to work on projects.

McGregor's Theory X and Theory Y A theory of motivation of staff which is based on the managers' perception of workers' attitudes to their work.

Medium-Term Finance Sources of money to acquire assets for a period of one to five years, namely hire purchase, leasing and term loans.

Memo A brief written message that is sent within an organisation, a copy of which is usually kept on file.

Memorandum Of Association A document which is produced for the formation of a limited company which gives details of the company name, address, its objectives, its share capital and its shareholders.

Merchandising The presentation and display of products in retail outlets to encourage consumers to buy the product.

Merchantable Quality Products sold by retailers must be of good enough quality to be sold to consumers under the Sale of Goods and Supply of Services Act 1980.

Merger When two businesses join together to form a new business.

Minutes A written record of what happened at a meeting and the decisions that were made, recorded by the secretary of the meeting.

Mortgage A long-term loan used to purchase a house where the house is used as security for the loan.

Motivating A management skill which uses various approaches to get staff to work hard for the business.

National Agreements Agreements between the government and social partners that cover wages, employment, taxation and other issues and usually last for a three-year period.

Negotiation A process where two or more parties with different objectives discuss what they want and finally make an agreement between them.

Net (Profit) Margin A profit calculation which expresses the net profit as a percentage of the value of the sales of the firm. Formula: net profit × sales × 100 = X %

Net Profit The profit made by a firm in a year after it has paid all the expenses of running the business.

Networking Refers to businesspeople getting to know as many people as possible in their business area so that they can use those contacts to help them in their business dealings in the future.

Niche Market A small segment in an overall market.

Non-Renewable Resources Raw materials that once used cannot be replaced, e.g. coal, natural gas.

Offer An element of a contract where one party sets out what they are willing to give to the other party as part of their agreement.

Official Dispute An industrial dispute that has the approval of the national executive of the union involved. This gives the dispute legal protection.

Ombudsman   An independent third party who will investigate a complaint against an organisation and make a recommendation to settle the complaint, e.g. the Ombudsman for the Public Service.

Operational Plan   A short-term plan to carry out a specific task, usually within a period of one year.

Organic Growth   When a business expands from within by increasing sales and reinvesting its profits in developing new products for the future.

Overdraft   A short-term loan from a bank operated through a current account. The account holder can take more money out of the account than was lodged up to an agreed limit.

Overtrading   This is when a firm does not have enough working capital to support a growing level of production and sales.

Partnership   Between two and twenty people owning and running a business together, sharing the risks, the work and the profits.

Pay As You Earn (PAYE) Income Tax   An income tax paid by all employees. It is calculated by the employer, deducted from wages and paid over to the Revenue Commissioners.

Pay Related Social Insurance (PRSI)   An insurance scheme operated by the government to provide unemployment benefits, maternity benefits and pensions to workers.

Performance Appraisal   Involves regular meetings between the manager and the employee to review the performance of the employee and to set objectives for the future.

Person Specification   A detailed description of the type of person wanted to fill a job vacancy, including the characteristics, qualifications, experience and skills required.

Picketing   Workers who are on strike publicise their dispute by gathering outside the workplace with protest signs.

Place   An element of the marketing mix for a product that focuses on the channels of distribution and outlets through which the product will be sold.

Policy   In insurance, a policy is a document setting out the details of the contract of insurance.

Polluter Pays Principle   When environmental damage has been done, the organisations responsible are made to correct the damage or pay for the necessary work.

Premium   In insurance, the money paid to the insurer for covering a risk is called the premium.

Pressure Groups   Groups of people or organisations who act together to influence or put pressure on decision-makers to make decisions favourable to their cause, e.g. Irish farmers trying to influence EU CAP reforms.

Price Discrimination   When companies charge different prices to different consumers for the same product in order to maximise their profits.

Primary Sector   Refers to industries in the economy that are based on natural resources, such as agriculture, mining, etc.

Private Limited Company   A form of business ownership where investors buy shares in the company, which becomes a separate legal entity that can sue and be sued.

Private Sector   The part of the economy which is not owned or controlled by the government.

Privatisation   The sale of a state-owned business by the government into private ownership.

Proactive   A businessperson is proactive if they anticipate things that may affect them in the future and act straight away rather than waiting and losing an advantage.

Product Liability Insurance   Protects a business from claims from its customers who suffer injury or loss resulting from faulty goods produced by the firm.

Product Life Cycle   Describes five stages in the life of a product from its introduction to the market to its withdrawal. Usually illustrated with a diagram.

Product Portfolio   Refers to a range of different products which a company may sell to various markets.

Product Positioning   Refers to how a firm will place its product among other competing products in the market in terms of quality, image, price, etc.

Productivity Agreement   A wage agreement between an employer and workers that allows pay rises which are dependent on increases in output achieved by workers.

Promotion   An element of the marketing mix where sales of the firm's products are developed through advertising, merchandising and other sales promotion techniques.

Protectionism   In international trade, this refers to countries blocking imports by using barriers to trade such as import taxes or subsidies to home producers.

Prototype   A working example of a proposed new product that proves the product can be made and allows the firm to test it and to work out costings for its manufacture.

Public Sector   The part of the economy which is in the control or ownership of the government.

Public Liability Insurance   Insurance which protects a firm against claims from members of the general public who suffer injury or loss as a result of visiting the premises of the firm.

Public Relations   Activities of a business aimed at enhancing the image of the firm with its customers and the general public. Activities may include press releases, press conferences, sponsoring charity events, company magazines, etc.

Public Relations Officer (PRO)   The person who speaks on behalf of an organisation or organises public relations activities.

Public-Private Partnerships   Development projects that are jointly owned by the state and private companies.

Quality Circles   Groups of employees from different parts of the business who are brought together to come up with ways of improving the quality of the products produced by the firm.

Quality Control   Refers to all efforts within the firm aimed at improving the quality of the products produced by the firm.

Ratio Analysis   The assessment of the financial performance of a firm by preparing and interpreting financial calculations (ratios) based on the firm's accounts.

Recruitment   The process of finding suitable candidates for positions in the business which need to be filled.

Redress   When a consumer buys faulty goods, they are entitled to a redress from the retailer to remedy their complaint. This may be a refund, a replacement or a repair.

Redundancy   Refers to an employee losing their job because the employer no longer has work for the employee.

Remuneration   The various forms of payments used to reward employees for the work that they do.

Renewable Resources   Raw material and sources of energy that can be replaced or renewed, allowing production to continue into the future, e.g. vegetable oils, wind power.

Research And Development (R&D)   Companies employ engineers and scientists to work to come up with new products, materials or ways of manufacturing which will ensure the success of the firm in the future.

Resource Audit   A survey in a community area to identify all the resources, human, physical and financial, which can be used for the economic and social development of the area.

Retailers   Businesses that sell products and services to consumers, usually shops.

Retained Earnings   The profit earned this year that still remains after tax has been paid to the government and dividends have been paid to the shareholders.

Return On Capital Employed (ROCE)   A measure of profitability for a firm which expresses the net profit of the firm as a percentage of the total capital used by the firm. Formula: net profit × capital employed × 100 = X %

Return On Investment (ROI)   See return on capital employed.

Revenue Commissioners   The term used for the government tax office that collects all taxes for the state.

Risk Management   Means eliminating and reducing risks so as to reduce the amount of insurance required and the cost of paying for insurance cover, e.g. install smoke alarms to reduce the risk of fire.

Sales Promotion   This covers various methods of encouraging people to buy a product, e.g. price reduction, free gift, saving stamps, free samples.

Secondary Sector   Refers to industries in the economy that convert raw materials into finished products, e.g. manufacturing and construction companies.

Secret Ballot   When members of a trade union are voting on whether to go on strike, the voting must be done so that no one knows how each individual has voted.

Seed Capital   Money invested in new companies starting up where the risks involved are high.

Self-Actualisation   One of the needs of workers identified by Maslow in his theory of motivation, which is the need to be challenged by your job and to achieve to the best of one's ability.

Semi-State Bodies   Companies that are owned and controlled by the government.

Service Providers   Firms that sell services to other firms in order to make a profit, e.g. transport firms.

Share Capital   The money raised by a limited company by selling shares to investors.

Shop Steward   An employee in an organisation who is elected by the union members in the workplace (shop) to represent them to management when industrial relations issues arise.

Short-Term Finance   Sources of money to finance the day-to-day running of a business over a period of less than one year, e.g. trade credit, bank overdraft.

Single European Market (SEM)   Refers to the EU policy of creation of a free market throughout all the member states with free movement of goods and services, capital and labour.

Small Claims Court   An inexpensive and speedy court procedure that can be used by consumers who have a complaint against a retailer.

Social Partners   A term used to refer to the participants in negotiations of national agreements with government, namely employers, employees (trade unions), farmers, the unemployed, voluntary and community organisations.

Social Responsibility   Refers to the duty of those running a business to look after the wider society in which they operate by being honest, fair, transparent, environmentally aware and considerate of their employees and customers.

Sole Trader   A business that is owned and run by one person.

Span Of Control   Refers to the number of subordinates that a member of staff manages or supervises directly.

Sponsorship   When companies provide money for sporting or charitable organisations in return for advertising or being publicly associated with their activities.

Staff Development   When a company prepares staff to take on greater responsibilities in the future by providing further training and courses to improve their skills and qualifications.

Staff Position   Is one which involves advising and giving support to other staff without having direct management responsibility for other staff, e.g. health and safety officer.

Stakeholders   All the individuals and organisations, both inside and outside the firm, who are affected by the decisions and actions of the firm, e.g. investors, employees, customers.

Standard Rate Cut-Off Point   The amount of a person's income which is subject to the standard rate of income tax.

Standing Orders   The agreed rules for the running of meetings in an organisation.

Stock Control   The methods and procedures used to ensure that a company's stock levels are at the optimum level for the efficient running of the business.

Stocktaking   On a chosen day, the stock of the firm is counted and its total value is calculated based on the cost price of the items held in stock.

Strategic Alliance (Joint Venture)   When two firms make an agreement to work together on a particular project while the companies still remain independent as businesses.

Strategic Plan   Sets out the means by which a firm will achieve its long-term objectives ranging over a five-year period or more.

Subrogation   A principle of insurance which states that if the insurer pays a claim in full the insurer then has the right to salvage any remaining part of the insured item or to sue any party responsible for the loss.

Subsidies   Payments given by the government to home producers of products so that they can compete on price with imported goods in their home market or in markets abroad when they export their products.

Sustainable Development   This refers to economic or business activity that does not adversely affect our capacity to produce goods in the future.

SWOT Analysis   This involves an examination of a situation based on identifying the strengths (S) and weaknesses (W) of the organisation internally and the opportunities (O) and threats (T) that the firm faces externally.

Target Market   A defined group of consumers that a particular product is aimed at.

Tax Credits   Reductions in the amount of tax payable by each individual. The amount allowed by the tax office depends on the circumstances of each tax payer.

Teamwork   Means people working together on a co-operative basis to achieve a shared objective. Having teamwork skills is very desirable in an employee.

Tele-working (E-work)   Refers to employees who do a lot of their work at home but who communicate with the office as needed using information and communications technology.

Term Loan   Borrowing from a bank for between one and five years with repayments made in instalments over the time period.

Tertiary Sector   Industries in the economy that provide services at a price, e.g. banks, entertainment providers.

Third-Party Insurance   A type of motor insurance that provides protection against claims by parties other than the insured for injuries caused by the insured person's car.

Total Quality Management   A constant system of improvement of quality in all aspects of the operation of a business to ensure customers' needs are fully met.

Trade Association   An organisation formed by all the firms in the same industry that will represent their interests, e.g. Society of the Irish Motor Industry (SIMI).

Trade Credit   When one company sells goods to another company and allows the buyer a period of time before they have to pay for the goods.

Trademark   An identifying name, slogan or logo for a business that is registered by the firm and cannot then be used by another business.

Transnational Corporation (TNC)   A company that manufactures and sells its products in a number of different countries.

Ultra Vires   When the directors of a company carry out business which is not provided for in the Memorandum of Association, the directors are said to be acting '*ultra vires*', e.g. outside their powers.

Unique Selling Point   A feature of a product which is highlighted by the firm as a reason to purchase it which other competing products do not have.

Unofficial Strike   A work stoppage by workers that does not have the approval of the trade union executive.

Urban Renewal   Refers to the rebuilding of parts of cities which have been in decline.

Utmost Good Faith   A principle of insurance that requires an applicant for insurance to be truthful in the information provided to the insurer.

Value-Added Tax (VAT)   A tax on the sale of goods and services that is paid by the consumer. The tax is collected for the Revenue Commissioners by businesses.

Variable Costs   The expenses of producing and selling a product which increase as the level of output increases, e.g. raw material and labour costs.

Venture Capital   The investment funds provided for starting up developing companies where the investment risk is high.

Visible Exports   Selling goods to foreign countries.

Visible Imports   Buying goods from foreign countries.

Warranty   A clause or part of a contract which if broken does not break the contract itself.

Wholesaler   A business that buys goods in large quantities from manufacturers and sells them in turn to retailers in smaller quantities.

Working Capital Ratio   See current ratio.

World-Class Manufacturing   Refers to firms producing products which are of such a high quality that they can compete with similar products from all over the world.

World Trade Organisation (WTO)   An organisation which has over 100 member countries who try to increase world trade levels by removing barriers to trade between countries.

World Wide Web   A network of websites containing information which can be accessed through the internet using a unique website address.